NAVIES OF THE SECOND WORLD WAR

AMERICAN SUBMARINES

H. T. LENTON

MACDONALD: LONDON

SBN 356 04190 5

First published in 1973 by
Macdonald & Co. (Publishers) Ltd.,
49 Poland Street, London W1.
Made and printed in Great Britain by
Redwood Press Limited
Trowbridge, Wiltshire

FOREWORD

Between the First and Second World Wars the United States Navy transformed its submarine service from a coast defence to an oceanic attack force owing to a steadily worsening relationship with Japan. With a forward main base in Hawaii and an advanced base in the Philippines the U.S.A. was strategically well situated, but it was always appreciated that the latter would be a prime target for Japanese attack as its long line of communications was vulnerable over practically its whole length. The defence of the Philippines was utterly dependent on maritime support, and that support could only be provided under the cover of the American battlefleet.

Even if measured from Hawaii the distances involved in the Pacific were vast, so that a large built-in radius was an essential requirement for all American warships. In one respect submarines were fortunate as they were powered by diesel engines—the most economical of marine prime movers—when surfaced, and could so enjoy a wide range of action on a modest bunkerage.

In the years following the First World War a programme of experimental submarine cruisers was put in hand, and after an initial upward surge unit size was progressively reduced. In conformity with standard practice these vessels were numbered only, but fish names were allocated to them in 1931 and all subsequent submarines were similarly named.

By the terms of the 1930 London Naval Treaty the U.S.A.—together with the U.K. and Japan—were limited to a total tonnage of 52,700 tons for submarines, none of which could exceed 2,000 tons standard in surfaced trim or carry a larger gun than of 5·1in (130mm) calibre (see *Note 1*). At the time the submarine strength of the United States Navy stood at one hundred and twenty-two boats of 81,039 tons plus five of 10,170 tons building, so that it was necessary to dispose of some 38,509 tons to comply with treaty limits. Hence, it was vital to keep unit size to the minimum compatible with operational requirements to secure the maximum number permitted by total tonnage (see *Note 2*). To further this end a diesel development programme was sponsored by the United States Navy, and weights were significantly reduced by adopting a fast-running unit. The end result was most gratifying as there was

---

Note 1: Special provision was made for the retention of submarines already completed which exceeded these limitations.
Note 2: While quantitative restrictions were abandoned under the 1936 London Naval Treaty the same qualitative restrictions still remained in force.

a choice of four suitable engines available for submarine propulsion. A fast-running diesel engine naturally prompted the selection of electric drive, especially as two units were required per shaft to obtain the requisite power output.

These new diesel engines were available for four prototypes laid down in 1933, two (*Porpoise* and *Pike*) to be built by Portsmouth Navy Yard and two (*Shark* and *Triton*) by Electric Boat, and from these boats it was a matter of steady development up to the outbreak of the Second World War. While geared diesel-electric drive was installed in the prototypes and the following production series, alternative drives were selected for the succeeding "Salmon"/ "Sargo" and "Tambor"/"Gar" classes so that all systems could be evaluated, but finally there was a reversion to diesel-electric drive owing to its all-round suitability.

War modifications to the SKIPJACK *include replacing the earlier 4-inch by a 5-inch deck gun and moving it to forward of the conning tower, and the addition of 20 mm A.A. guns and GW.RDF*   [Photograph U.S. Navy

4

On the American entry into the Second World War submarine strength stood at one hundred and thirteen boats, of which sixty-four belonged to the old "O"/"R"/"S" coastal types, nine were large experimental submarine cruisers, and only forty were of modern construction (thirty-eight ocean-going and two coastal units). Under construction, however, were thirty-two boats of the "Gato" class, and a further forty-one were authorised.

Submarine construction—a small and highly specialised field—had shrunk to only three builders: Portsmouth and Mare Island Navy Yards and Electric Boat, therefore any large scale production had to be tempered by the limited building facilities available. The position was far more satisfactory with the supply of propulsion machinery and sub-contract equipment which American industry could absorb without any great difficulty when switched to war production.

The decision was wisely made to adhere to the all-welded *Gato* design for war construction, and bearing in mind the other large programmes put in hand for all types of warships the output was impressive. Under the stimulus of war conditions two other commercial builders and one other Navy Yard undertook submarine construction, but the bulk of the work was undertaken by Electric Boat and Portsmouth Navy Yard as summarised in the table below:

Builder/Class	"Gato"	"Balao"	"Tench"	SS.551	Totals
Electric Boat	41	46 (8)	3 (23)	— (5)	90 (36)
Portsmouth N.Y.	14	42	24 (28)	— (5)	80 (33)
Mare Island N.Y.	8	4	— (6)	— (2)	12 (8)
Manitowoc	10	18 (2)	— (17)	—	28 (19)
Cramp	—	12	2 (15)	—	14 (15)
Boston N.Y.	—	—	4 (12)	—	4 (12)
Totals	73	122 (10)	33 (101)	— (12)	228 (123)

Note: Cancelled contracts are shown in parentheses.

A total of sixty submarines were lost from all causes: sixteen of them by circumstances unknown at the time but on which Japanese records have since shed some light although five still remain a complete mystery. A summary

In this early war view the CUTTLEFISH *is unaltered, and it illustrates the extensive deck casing typical of American submarines*   [Photograph U.S. Navy

of the cause of loss is shown in the accompanying table. These losses were principally incurred in a relentless campaign directed against Japanese trade which exacted a heavy toll: some 4,000,000 tons gross of enemy shipping was sunk, together with a significant number of warships. On a percentage basis submarine losses were high when compared with other categories of American warships, but they were considerably lower than those sustained by Axis submarines.

Cause	Number
Bombed	9
Gunfire	2
Depth charged	17½
Torpedoed	1
Mined	7½
Unknown	5
Miscellaneous	.18
Total	60

At the close of the war the Japanese furnished the United States Navy with a report listing the sinking of four hundred and eighty-six American submarines, and they had clearly been lulled into a sense of false security with regards the effectiveness of the A/S measures. In actual fact not more than forty-two submarines were lost as a direct result of enemy action, and the strict American censorship on the activities of their submarines contributed in no small manner to keeping the Japanese in the dark.

The installation of RDF greatly assisted American submarines in their operations, as they were less prone to be surprised on the surface by ships and aircraft and were not wholly dependent on visual sighting for detecting targets. By mid-1942 all boats had been equipped with AW.RDF, and by the end of the year with SW.RDF as well. Later, RDF detecting equipment was fitted to counter the use of RDF in Japanese vessels, and when the Japanese installed similar equipment this was countered by the production of new warning sets operating on shorter wavelengths. There can be no doubt that in the electronic field the Japanese were at a severe disadvantage.

When it is considered that the United States Navy had little expertise in waging submarine warfare then their success in this sphere is all the more remarkable. The essential nucleus—efficient and reliable submarines manned by well-trained crews—was created pre-war, but no peacetime exercises could realistically simulate war conditions and combat experience had to be accumulated the hard way. Above all, the prime object of the American submarine campaign—to seek out and sink ship targets—was never lost to sight despite other calls made on their services.

I am particularly indebted to the Public Affairs and Historical Departments of the United States Navy for their generous assistance with information and photographs, and to Mr. Samuel L. Morison and Mr. Stephen Roberts for their valuable collaboration and research.

H.T.L.

Ewelme, 1971.

Hull No.	Name	Builder	Launched	Fate
SS.63	O.2	Puget Sound N.Y. (Bremerton)	24.5.18	Sold North American Smelting (Philadelphia) 16/11/45 & scrapped.
SS.64	O.3	Fore River (Quincy)	29.9.17	Sold John J. Duane Co. (Quincy) 4/9/46 & scrapped.
SS.65	O.4	,,	20.10.17	Sold . . . . (. . . . .) 2/1/46 & scrapped.
SS.67	O.6	,,	25.11.17	Sold John J. Duane Co. (Quincy) 4/9/46 & scrapped.
SS.68	O.7	,,	16.12.17	Sold North American Smelting (Philadelphia) 22/1/46 & scrapped.
SS.69	O.8	,,	31.12.17	Sold John J. Duane Co. (Quincy) 4/9/46 & scrapped.
SS.70	O.9	,,	27.1.18	Foundered off Isle of Shoals 20/6/41.
SS.71	O.10	,,	21.2.18	Sold John J. Duane Co. (Quincy) 21/8/46 & scrapped.

Machinery contracts: All engined by New London Ship & Engine (diesel engines); and by Electro Dynamic (electric motors).

Early American submarine design followed a generally evolutionary pattern with slight improvements in each suc- ceeding class. In 1916 design stabilised on the "N" class which reverted to slightly reduced dimensions and machinery of less installed power but greater reliability. With few exceptions submarines were built to the design of Holland or Lake to meet general characteristics framed by the United States Navy.

The upward trend in submarine development was continued with the "O" class which were of the usual two saddle tank designs: the first ten (*O.1–10*) being of the Holland type, and the last six (*O.11–16*) of the Lake type. However, to familiarise itself with submarine construction the U.S. Navy placed the first two Holland contracts with Navy Yards, and these were the first tentative steps taken by them to provide their own designs.

The *O.5* was accidentally lost in 1923, the *O.11–16* were scrapped in 1930, and the *O.1* scrapped in 1938. All boats had originally been fitted with a 3in gun on deck, forward of the conning tower, but this had been removed in the surviving units by the outbreak of the Second World War. As they were built for coast defence duties they had a limited radius of action, and were principally used for training purposes during the war.

Displacement:	521/629 tons.
Dimensions:	164(wl) 172¼(oa) × 18 × 14½ feet.
Machinery:	Two shafts; NLSE diesel engines & Electro Dynamic electric motors, B.H.P./S.H.P. 880/740 = 14/10½ knots.
Bunkers & radius:	88 tons/120-cell Exide except *O.2* Gould battery; .,....../... miles @ ../.. knots.
Armament:	One ·5-inch A.A. machine gun; four 18-inch (all fixed & fwd—eight torpedoes) T.T.
Complement:	32.
Diving depth;	200 feet.

Pre-war view of the O.6 (SS.67) in surface trim with W/T aerials rigged. No deck gun is fitted but a heavy A.A. machine gun can be shipped at the after end of the conning tower

[Photograph
U.S. Navy

Pre-war view of the R.1 *(SS.78) in surface trim and with only a single W/T mast admidships to spread the aerials.*
Note that name and not hull number is painted-up on the conning tower   [Photograph U.S. Navy

Hull No.	Name	Builder	Launched	Fate
SS.78	*R.1*	Fore River (Quincy)	24.8.18	Sold Macy O. Scott (Miami) 13/3/46 & scrapped.
SS.79	*R.2*	,,	23.9.18	Sold Rosoff Bros. (New York) 28/10/45, resold Northern Metals (Philadelphia) & scrapped.
SS.80	*R.3*	,,	18.1.19	R.N. *P.511* (1941); returned U.S.N. 20/12/44, broke adrift Kames Bay 27/11/47 & written-off as constructive total loss, sold West of Scotland Sbkg. (Troon) ../12/47 & scrapped.
SS.81	*R.4*	,,	26.10.18	Sold North American Smelting (Philadelphia) 22/1/46 & scrapped.
SS.82	*R.5*	,,	24.11.18	Sold John J. Duane Co. (Quincy) 22/8/46 & scrapped.
SS.83	*R.6*	,,	1.3.19	Sold Macy O. Scott (Miami) 13/3/46 & scrapped.
SS.84	*R.7*	,,	5.4.19	Sold John J. Duane Co. (Quincy) 4/9/46 & scrapped.
SS.86	*R.9*	,,	24.5.19	Sold . . . . (. . . . .) 1/2/46 & scrapped.

The R.1 *(above) and the* R.8 *(below) pre-war*

Hull No.	Name	Builder	Launched	Fate
SS.87	*R.10*	Fore River (Quincy)	28.6.19	Sold North American Smelting (Philadelphia) 22/1/46 & scrapped.
SS.88	*R.11*	,,	21.7.19	Sold Macy O. Scott (Miami) 13/3/46 & scrapped.
SS.89	*R.12*	,,	15.8.19	Foundered off Key West 12/6/43.
SS.90	*R.13*	,,	27.8.19	Sold Macy O. Scott (Miami) 13/3/46 & scrapped.
SS.91	*R.14*	,,	10.10.19	Sold Rosoff Bros. (New York) 28/10/45, resold Northern Metals (Philadelphia) & scrapped.
SS.92	*R.15*	Union I.W. (San Francisco)	10.12.17	Sold Macy O. Scott (Miami) 13/3/46 & scrapped.
SS.93	*R.16*	,,	15.12.17	Sold North American Smelting (Philadelphia) 22/1/46 & scrapped.
SS.94	*R.17*	,,	24.12.17	R.N. *P.512* (1942); returned U.S.N. 6/9/44, sold North American Smelting (Philadelphia) 16/11/45 & scrapped.
SS.95	*R.18*	,,	8.1.18	Sold John J. Duane Co. (Quincy) 4/9/46 & scrapped).

This class was slightly lengthened to accommodate the larger 21in T.T.; and the first twenty (*R.1–20*) were built to the Holland design, and the last seven (*R.21–27*) to the Lake design. The latter were all scrapped in 1930 and the *R.8* in 1936. Like the "O" class they were principally used for training, and three units—the *R.13*, *R.17*, and *R.19*—were loaned to the Royal Navy during 1941–42 for a similar purpose.

Displacement:	569/680 tons.
Dimensions:	179(wl) 186¼(oa) × 18 × 14½ feet.
Machinery:	Two shafts; NLSE diesel engines and Electro Dynamic electric motors B.H.P./S.H.P. 1,200/934 = 13½/10½ knots.
Bunkers & *radius:*	O.F. 75 tons/120-cell Exide battery; 4,000/... miles @ 10/.. knots.
Armament:	One 3-inch/50cal gun; four 21-inch (all fixed & fwd—eight torpedoes) T.T.
Complement:	33.
Diving depth:	200 feet.

Hull No.	Name	Builder	Launched	Fate
SS.96	*R.19*	Union I.W. (San Francisco)	28.1.18	R.N. *P.514* (1942); collision R.C.N. minesweeper *Georgian* North Atlantic 21/6/42.
SS.97	*R.20*	,,	21.1.18	Sold Macy O. Scott (Miami) 13/3/46 & scrapped.

Machinery contracts: All engined by New London Ship & Engine (diesel engines); and by Electro Dynamic (electric motors).

Hull No.	Name	Builder	Launched	Fate
SS.105	*S.1*	Fore River (Quincy)	26.10.18	R.N. *P.552* (1942); sold .... (Durban) 30/7/45 & scrapped.
SS.116	*S.11*	Portsmouth N.Y.	7.2.21	Sold Rosoff Bros. (New York) 28/10/45, resold Northern Metals (Philadelphia) & scrapped.
SS.117	*S.12*	,,	4.8.21	Sold Rosoff Bros (New York) 28/10/45, resold Northern Metals (Philadelphia) & scrapped.
SS.118	*S.13*	,,	20.10.21	Sold Rosoff Bros. (New York) 28/10/45, resold Northern Metals (Philadelphia) & scrapped.
SS.119	*S.14*	Lake Torpedo Boat (Bridgeport)	22.10.19	Sold North American Smelting (Philadelphia) 16/11/45 & scrapped.
SS.120	*S.15*	,,	8.3.20	Sold Potomac Shwg. Co. (Pope's Creek) 4/12/46 & scrapped.
SS.121	*S.16*	,,	23.12.19	Expended as target off Key West 3/4/45.
SS.122	*S.17*	,,	22.5.20	Expended as target off .... 5/4/45.

The three prototypes were all built to the same military characteristics but to Holland (*S.1*), Lake (*S.2*), and Bureau of Construction & Repair (*S.3*) designs: the last being the first submarine designed by the United States Navy. As the Bureau design was considered superior to that of Lake the latter was finally dropped, and the production series adopted either Bureau (*S.4–17*) or Holland (*S.18–41*) designs. A second Holland (*S.42–47*) and Bureau (*S.48–51*) series had dimensions increased to improve endurance.

Compared with the "O"/"R" classes these boats were enlarged to have a wider sphere of action, a higher sustained surface speed, and stow more torpedo reloads; and an additional stern T.T. was worked into eight units (*S.10–13* and *48–51*). In 1923 the *S.1* was experimentally provided with a seaplane, and four similar units were completed for the Peruvian Navy during 1926–28. Prior to the outbreak of the Second World War the *S.4*, the *S.5*, and the *S.51* were accidentally lost; and the *S.2*, *S.3*, *S.6–10*, *S.19*, *S.49*, and *S.50* were scrapped.

In the early period of the war a few units stationed in the Far East were used for offensive patrols, but after the loss of the Philippines they possessed insufficient range for employment in the Pacific. Although used for a limited amount of patrol work in other areas where distance was less critical the class was otherwise mainly used for training, and with the large war programmes put in hand for A/S vessels and submarines the importance of the training role need hardly be emphasised.

Five units of this type—the *S.1*, *S.21*, *S.22*, *S.24*, and *S.25*—were loaned to the Royal Navy between 1942–44, and after sporadic employment as convoy escorts were also used for training.

SS.123	*S.18*	Bethlehem (Quincy)	29.4.20	Sold . . . . (. . . . .) 9/11/46 & scrapped.
SS.125	*S.20*	,,	9.6.20	Sold North American Smelting (Philadelphia) 22/1/46 & scrapped.
SS.126	*S.21*	,,	18.8.20	R.N. *P.553* (1942); scuttled as A/S target off . . . . 20/3/45.

Hull No.	Name	Builder	Launched	Fate
SS.127	*S.22*	Bethlehem (Quincy)	15.7.20	R.N. *P.554* (1942); sold North American Smelting (Philadelphia) 16/11/45 & scrapped.
SS.128	*S.23*	,,	27.10.20	Sold . . . . (. . . . .) 9/11/46 and scrapped.
SS.129	*S.24*	,,	27.6.22	R.N. *P.555* (1942); scuttled as A/S target off Portland 25/8/47.
SS.130	*S.25*	,,	29.5.22	R.N. *P.551* (1941); Polish Navy *Jastrzab* (1942); depth charged in error by R.N. destroyer *St. Albans* and minesweeper *Seagull* off North Norway 2/5/42.
SS.131	*S.26*	,,	22.8.22	Collision sub-chaser *PC.460* Gulf of Panama 24/1/42.
SS.132	*S.27*	,,	18.10.22	Wrecked Amchitka Island 19/6/42.
SS.133	*S.28*	,,	20.9.22	Lost—cause unknown—off Pearl Harbour 4/7/44.
SS.134	*S.29*	,,	9.11.22	R.N. *P.556* (1942); stranded Portchester . ./1/47, sold H. G. Pounds (Portsmouth) 24/1/47, salved . . / . . /65 & scrapped.

Unlike the "R" class the 4-inch gun was housed trained forward in the "S" class, as illustrated by the S.1 *(SS.105)*

[Photographs N.M.M.

First group

Displacement:	854/1,062 tons.
Dimensions:	211(wl) 219¼(oa) × 20¾ × 16 feet.
Machinery:	Two shafts; NLSE diesel engines & Electro Dynamic (*S.1 & 30–35*)/Ridgway (*S.18, 20–29*)/General Electric (*S.36–41*) electric motors B.H.P./S.H.P. 1,200/1,500 = 14½/11 knots.
Bunkers & radius:	O.F. 168 tons/120-cell Exide battery; .,.../... miles @ ../.. knots.
Armament:	One 4-inch/50cal gun; four 21-inch (all fixed & fwd—twelve torpedoes) T.T.
Complement:	42.
Diving depth:	200 feet.

Hull No.	Name	Builder	Launched	Fate
SS.135	*S.30*	Bethlehem (San Francisco)	21.11.18	Sold Salco Iron & Metal (San Francisco) 5/12/46 & scrapped.
SS.136	*S.31*	,,	28.12.18	Sold Salco Iron & Metal (San Francisco) 6/12/46 & scrapped.
SS.137	*S.32*	,,	11.1.19	Sold Learner Co. (Oakland) 19/4/46 & scrapped.
SS.138	*S.33*	,,	5.12.18	Sold Salco Iron & Metal (San Francisco) 5/12/46 & scrapped.
SS.139	*S.34*	,,	13.2.19	Sold Salco Iron & Metal (San Francisco) 23/11/46 & scrapped.
SS.140	*S.35*	,,	27.2.19	Expended as target off . . . . 4/4/46.
SS.141	*S.36*	,,	3.6.19	Wrecked off Taka Bakang Reef (Makassar Strait) 20/1/42 and scuttled following day.
SS.142	*S.37*	,,	20.6.19	Scuttled off San Diego 20/2/45.
SS.143	*S.38*	,,	17.6.19	Scuttled off San Diego 20/2/45.
SS.144	*S.39*	,,	2.7.19	Wrecked off Rossel Island 13–14/8/42.

Note different shape of the conning tower of the S.11 *(second group) compared with* S.1 *(first group)*

Second group

Displacement:	876/1,092 tons.
Dimensions:	231(wl) 231(oa) × 21¾ × 13 feet.
Machinery:	Two shafts; M.A.N. (*S.11–13*)/Busch-Sulzer (*S.14–17*) diesel engines & Westinghouse electric motors B.H.P./S.H.P. 2,000/1,200 = 15/11 knots.
Bunkers & radius:	O.F. 148 tons/120-cell Exide battery; .,..../... miles @ ../.. knots.
Armament:	As in *first group* except *S.11–13* five 21-inch (four fwd & one aft—fourteen torpedoes) T.T.
Complement and *Diving depth:*	As in *first group*.

Hull No.	Name	Builder	Launched	Fate
SS.145	S.40	Bethlehem (San Francisco)	5.1.21	Sold Salco Iron & Metal (San Francisco) 19/11/46 & scrapped.
SS.146	S.41	,,	21.2.21	Sold National Metal & Steel (Terminal Island) 15/11/46 & scrapped.
SS.147	S.42	Bethlehem (Quincy)	30.4.23	Sold Salco Iron & Metal (San Francisco) 23/11/46 & scrapped.
SS.148	S.43	,,	31.3.23	Sold Salco Iron & Metal (San Francisco) 7/12/46 & scrapped.
SS.149	S.44	,,	27.10.23	Gunfire I.J.N. destroyer east of Kamchatka Peninsula 7/10/43.
SS.150	S.45	,,	26.6.23	Sold Salco Iron & Metal (San Francisco) 6/12/46 & scrapped.
SS.151	S.46	,,	11.9.23	Sold Salco Iron & Metal (San Francisco) 19/11/46 & scrapped.
SS.152	S.47	,,	5.1.24	Sold Salco Iron & Metal (San Francisco) 22/11/46 & scrapped.
SS.153	S.48	,,	26.2.21	Sold North American Smelting (Philadelphia) 22/1/46 & scrapped.

Third group

Displacement:	906/1,126 tons.
Dimensions:	216(wl) 225¼(oa) × 20¾ × 16 feet.
Machinery:	As in *first group* except Electro Dynamic electric motors in all.
Bunkers & radius:	O.F. 185 tons/120-cell Exide battery; .,.../... miles @ ../.. knots.
Armament:	As in *first group*.
Complement and *Diving depth:*	As in *first group*.

Fourth group

Displacement:	903/1,230 tons.
Dimensions:	240(wl) 266(oa) × 21¾ × 13½ feet.
Machinery:	Two shafts; Busch-Sulzer diesel engines & Ridgway electric motors B.H.P./S.H.P. 1,800/1,500 = 14½/11 knots.
Bunkers & radius:	O.F. 177 tons/120-cell Gould battery; ...../... miles @ ../.. knots.
Armament:	One 4-inch/50cal gun; five 21-inch (four fwd & one aft—fourteen torpedoes) T.T.
Complement and *Diving depth:*	As in *first group*.

Machinery contracts: All engined by New London Ship & Engine except *S.11–13* New York N.Y. and *S.14–17* and *S.48* Busch-Sulzer (diesel engines); and by Electro Dynamic except *S.11–17* Westinghouse, *S.18*, *S.20–29* and *S.48* Ridgway, and *S.36–41* General Electric (electric motors).

Above: Note different conning tower of S.47 (third group) compared with the first and second groups of this class. Left: Pre-war views of S.43 (top) and S.44 (bottom): both third group. Below: Pre-war view of the S.48 (fourth group)

Experimental type: **ONE** unnamed unit

Interposed between the "S" class prototypes (SS.105–107) and the production series (SS.109 up) was an unnamed experimental unit (SS.108). This boat was authorised in 1916, and was to be equipped with the Neff system of propulsion, ans was to be a coast defence unit of about 150 tons submerged, armed similarly to the "C" class (two 18in T.T.).

The Neff system entailed using the diesel engine while submerged with compressed air used for the combustion cycle. By these means it was hoped to increase submerged speed and radius by eliminating the electric motors and storage batteries. A problem involved with this system was the disposal of the excess combustion products, which absorbed an appreciable amount of power—proportional to the depth—for the compressor. This interesting project was abandoned, however, and the boat never built.

"T" class: **T.1–3**

This class of large submarines were completed in 1920–22 to a Holland design, and with displacements of 1,107/1,482 tons were considerably larger than pervious American boats. They were originally numbered *AA.1–3* (SS.52, 60 & 61) and chronologically preceded the "O"/"R"/"S" classes, but were re-numbered *T.1–3* (SF.1–3). in 1920. They were of the usual saddle tank type, and as they did not prove very successful in service owing to mechanical unreliability were scrapped in 1930.

"V" class: **V.1–9**

After the First World War there was a shift of concentration from the Atlantic to the Pacific for the United States Navy; and while some of the larger coast defence submarines could (and did) undertake an Atlantic crossing, the

Right: Pre-war view of the BONITA *showing distinctive bow*   [Photograph N.M.M.

vast distances involved in the Pacific entailed a much larger unit to possess the necessary endurance. Immediate post-war construction, therefore, was concentrated on a series of submarine cruisers modelled on the German units of this type together with experience gained with the "T" class. These vessels were initially numbered *V.1–9* but were given fish names in 1931, which subsequently became standard nomenclature for American submarines. Under both systems of numbering and naming they adopted distinctive pendant numbers different from the hull numbers allocated to all construction from 1920, but

Hull No.	No. (Pendant No.)	Name (Pendant No.)
SS.163	*V.1* (SF.4)	*Barracuda* (B.1)
SS.164	*V.2* (SF.5)	*Bass* (B.2)
SS.165	*V.3* (SF.6)	*Bonita* (B.3)
SS.166	*V.4* (SF.7 = SM.1)	*Argonaut* (A.1)
SS.167	*V.5* (SF.8 = SC.1)	*Narwhal* (N.1)
SS.168	*V.6* (SF.9 = SC.2)	*Nautilus* (N.2)
SS.169	*V.7* (SF.10 = SC.3)	*Dolphin* (D.1)
SS.170	*V.8* (SF.11 = SC.4)	*Cachalot* (C.1)
SS.171	*V.9* (SF.12 = SC.5)	*Cuttlefish* (C.2)

by the outbreak of the Second World War these special pendant numbers had been dropped in favour of the original hull numbers. The changes of names and numbers, often the subject of some confusion, are detailed in the accompanying table.

The deck gun has been removed from the BASS, *and two 20 mm A.A. guns and GW.RDF added*   [Photographs U.S. Navy

Hull No.	Name	Builder	Launched	Fate
SS.163	*Barracuda* (ex-*V.1*)	Portsmouth N.Y.	17.7.24	Sold North American Smelting (Philadelphia) 16/11/45 & scrapped.
SS.164	*Bass* (ex-*V.2*)	,,	27.12.24	Expended as target North Atlantic 12/3/45, salved, sold Nicholas Zinkowski (Newport) . ./6/63 & scrapped.
SS.165	*Bonita* (ex-*V.3*)	,,	9.6.25	Sold Rosoff Bros. (New York) 28/10/45, resold Northern Metals (Philadelphia) & scrapped.

Machinery contracts: Engined by Busch-Sulzer and New York N.Y. (diesel engines), and Elliot Motor (electric motors)

Barracuda, Bass and Bonita

To secure good surface qualities these prototypes were of double-hull construction, and most of the extra size was accounted for by more powerful machinery, increased bunker capacity, and improved habitability. There was no virtual increase in torpedo armament as despite the additional stern tubes only twelve torpedoes were carried: the same as in the "S" class, but a heavier 5in gun was shipped in the *Barracuda* and the *Bonita* while the *Bass* shipped a lighter 3in gun.

Main propulsion was on the composite drive system with two diesel engines coupled direct to the shafts, and two other units driving generators which supplied power to the electric motors while surfaced. Although the system was satisfactory they never made their designed surfaced speed of 21 knots, and were partially re-engined pre-war when the original Sulzer generating diesel engines were replaced by M.A.N. units with a higher output.

During the war it was proposed to convert them to transport submarines (APS.2–4) after withdrawal from front-line service, but this was not finally implemented.

Displacement:	2,000/2,620 tons.
Dimensions:	326(wl) 341½(oa) × 27½ × 14½ feet.
Machinery:	Two shafts; 6-cylinder Busch-Sulzer & 10-cylinder M.A.N. diesel engines (two/shaft) & Elliot electric motors B.H.P./S.H.P. 6,700/2,400 = 18/8 knots.
Bunkers & radius:	O.F. 364 tons/120-cell Exide except *Bonita* Gould battery; 12,000/... miles @ ../.. knots.
Armament:	One 5-inch/51cal except *Bass* 3-inch/50cal, two machine (2 × 1) guns; six 21-inch (four fwd & two aft—twelve torpedoes) T.T.
Complement:	80.
Diving depth:	200 feet.

Above: Early war view of the BONITA. *Below: Pre-war view of the* ARGONAUT *with deck sponsoned-out to accommodate 6-inch guns*

[Photograph U.S. Navy

Argonaut

This vessel was an enlarged version of the *Barracuda* modified to serve as a minelayer. The bunker and battery capacity was doubled to widen both the surfaced and submerged radius, the after T.T. were omitted so that two minelaying chutes could be provided at the stern, the reload capacity was increased to sixteen torpedoes, and the gun armament strengthened; but there was a reduction in installed power and speed.

For her day the *Argonaut* was most completely fitted to wage trade warfare—by gun, torpedo, or mine—in distant waters, but paid the penalty in size and loss of manoeuvrability submerged although this was partly offset by the deeper depth to which she could submerge. As the main machinery (composite drive) proved unreliable it was planned to re-engine the *Argonaut* with General Motors diesel engines in 1940–41, but war intervened and she was converted to a supply submarine (APS.1) instead.

Displacement:	2,710/4,164 tons.
Dimensions:	358(wl) 381(oa) × 33¾ × 15¼ feet.
Machinery:	Two shafts; 6-cyl M.A.N. diesel engines & Ridgway electric motors B.H.P./S.H.P. 3,175/2,400 = 15/8 knots.
Bunkers & radius:	O.F. 696 tons/240-cell Exide battery; ..,..../... miles @ ../... knots.
Armament:	Two 6-inch/53cal (2 × 1), two ·3-inch (2 × 1) guns; four 21-inch (all fwd—sixteen torpedoes) T.T., sixty mines.
Complement:	89.
Diving depth:	300 feet.

SS.166	*Argonaut* (i) (ex-*V.4*)	Portsmouth N.Y.	10.11.27	APS.1 (1942); depth charged and gunfire I.J.N. destroyers south-east of New Britain 10/1/43.

Machinery contract: Engined by New York N.Y. (diesel engines), and Ridgway (electric motors).

War modifications to the NARWHAL *included the addition of external T.T. forward, 20 mm A.A. guns forward and aft of the conning tower, and GW.RDF; while the W/T mast has been re-sited abaft the periscope standard. Note partially raised spar deck for 6-inch guns*

[Photograph U.S. Navy

Narwhal, Nautilus

These vessels were generally similar to the *Argonaut* except that they were not equipped for minelaying so that the torpedo armament could be strengthened. As a result the aft T.T. were re-introduced, eight reloads were carried externally under the gun casings forward and aft, and installed power and speed were increased to better suit them for patrol work. Both were re-engined in 1940–41 when their original M.A.N. diesel engines were replaced by Fairbanks Morse units, and composite by diesel-electric drive. During the war four external T.T.—two forward and two aft—were added in place of the external reloads, the after tubes being abaft the conning tower in the *Nautilus* but well aft in the *Narwhal*.

Displacement:	2,730/4,050 tons.
Dimensions:	349(wl) 371(oa) × 33¼ × 15¾ feet.
Machinery:	Two shafts; Fairbanks Morse diesel engines (two/shaft)/Westinghouse electric motors B.H.P./S.H.P. 5,400/2,540 = 17/8 knots.
Bunkers & *radius:*	O.F. 732 tons/240-cell Exide battery; ..,..../... miles @ ../.. knots.
Armament:	Two 6-inch/53cal (2 × 1), two ·3-inch (2 × 1) guns; six 21-inch (four fwd & two aft—twenty-four torpedoes) T.T.
Complement:	90.
Diving depth:	300 feet.

SS.167	*Narwhal* (ex-*V*.5)	Portsmouth N.Y.	17.12.29	Sold North American Smelting (Philadelphia) 16/11/45 & scrapped.
SS.168	*Nautilus* (ex-*V*.6)	Mare Island N.Y. (Vallejo)	15.3.30	Sold North American Smelting (Philadelphia) 16/11/45 & scrapped.

Machinery contracts: Re-engined by Fairbanks Morse (diesel engines), and Westinghouse (electric motors).

Above: Early war view of the NAUTILUS. *Below: Pre-war view of the* DOLPHIN *wearing non-standard pendant number*

[Photographs U.S. Navy

Dolphin

Except for a reduction in gun armament this vessel otherwise attempted to combine the military characteristics of the preceding pair on practically half the displacement. To save weight the *Dolphin* reverted to saddle-tank construction, adopted lighter scantlings, and carried less bunkers; and while she did not prove a great success was a positive step in the direction to reduce unit size. She was mainly used for training during the war.

Displacement:	1,560/2,240 tons.
Dimensions:	307(wl) 319¼(oa) × 27¾ × 13¼ feet.
Machinery:	Two shafts; 6-cylinder M.A.N. diesel engines (two/shaft)/Electro Dynamic electric motors B.H.P./ S.H.P. 3,500/1,750 = 17/8 knots.
Bunkers & radius:	O.F. 412 tons/240-cell Gould battery; ....../... miles @ ../.. knots.
Armament:	One 4-inch/50cal, four ·3-inch (4 × 1) guns; six 21-inch (four fwd & two aft—eighteen torpedoes) T.T.
Complement:	60.
Diving depth:	250 feet.

Hull No.	Name	Builder	Launched	Fate
SS.169	*Dolphin* (ex-*V*.7)	Portsmouth N.Y.	6.3.32	Sold John J. Duane Co. (Quincy) 26/8/46 & scrapped.

Machinery contract: Engined by New York N.Y. (diesel engines), and Electro Dynamic (electric motors).

Pre-war view of the CACHALOT *(above) with deck gun abaft the conning tower; and the* CUTTLEFISH *(below) with the deck gun moved to forward of the conning tower and other war modifications* [Photographs U.S. Navy

Cachalot, Cuttlefish

Size was further reduced with these units, but except for some loss of bunker capacity they otherwise retained the same military features of the *Dolphin*. The hull was of all-welded construction, and with this technique the United States Navy was well ahead of other navies which enabled saving in weight for a constructionally stronger pressure hull. While the original M.A.N. diesel engines were directly coupled to the shafts, the drive was taken through reduction gearing when re-engined with fast-running units.

War modifications included reducing the conning tower structure in size and arranging platforms forward and aft of it for two 20mm A.A. (2 × 1) guns, and re-mounting the 3in gun forward of the conning tower from its original position abaft it. Both units were only briefly employed operationally before taking up training duties.

Displacement:	*Cachalot* 1,110 & *Cuttlefish* 1,130/1,650 tons.
Dimensions:	260(wl) *Cachalot* 271¾/*Cuttlefish* 274(oa) × 24¾ × 13 feet.
Machinery:	Two shafts; General Motors diesel engines & Electro Dynamic (*Cachalot*)/Westinghouse (*Cuttlefish*) electric motors B.H.P./S.H.P. 3,100/1,600 = 17/8 knots.
Bunkers & radius:	O.F. 333 tons/240-cell Exide battery; ..,..../... miles @ ../.. knots.
Armament:	One 3-inch/50cal, four ·3-inch (4 × 1) guns; six 21-inch (four fwd & two aft—sixteen torpedoes) T.T.
Complement:	50.
Diving depth:	250 feet.

SS.170	*Cachalot* (ex-*V.8*)	Portsmouth N.Y.	19.10.33	Sold Ship-Shape Inc. (Philadelphia) 26/1/47 & scrapped.
SS.171	*Cuttlefish* (ex-*V.9*)	Electric Boat (Groton)	21.11.33	Sold Ship-Shape Inc. (Philadelphia) 12/2/47 & scrapped.

Machinery contracts: Re-engined by General Motors (diesel engines), and Westinghouse (electric motors).

"Porpoise" class: First group **PIKE, PORPOISE.** *Second group* **SHARK, TARPON.** *Third group* **PERCH, PERMIT, PICKEREL, PLUNGER, POLLACK, POMPANO**

Reduction in size had been taken a little too far with the preceding *Cachalot*, but sufficient experience had now been accumulated to show the feasibility of a 1,500-ton submarine suitable for Pacific operations, so that with this class there were modest increases in size to improve internal arrangements and take advantage of a naval sponsored diesel development programme.

To secure increased power with less weight the broad specifications given to engine manufacturers were for a fast-running diesel engine of not less than 700 r.p.m. with solid injection of fuel and suitable for mass production. Both Winton (later absorbed by General Motors) and General Motors had responded with suitable prototypes; and were later joined by Hooven, Owens, Rentschler (HOR) and Fairbanks Morse so that a choice of four suitable engines were available. The higher speed of these units ruled out coupling them direct to the shaft so that the drive had to be diesel-electric or through reduction gearing.

Electric drive was selected for the first and second groups with two pairs of diesel generators supplying power to each line of shafting. As space was not available for a single large electric motor two smaller fast-running units were coupled to each shaft through gearing, and the whole arrangement proved very versatile as one or all the diesel engines could be operated according to choice and the maintenance load evenly spread. A similar arrangement was adopted

The PIKE *pre-war in surface trim with* W/T *aerials rigged and the deck gun abaft the conning tower*

for the lengthened third group except that the first three boats had four electric motors coupled to each shaft through reduction gearing.

They were originally allocated the pendant numbers S.1–10, but by the outbreak of war had adopted standard hull numbers. All groups were armed as the *Cachalot* but a 4in gun was shipped abaft the conning tower in the second and third groups. During the war the conning tower was reduced in size and modified so that two 20mm A.A. (2 × 1) guns could be mounted (one forward and one aft); and two external bow T.T. were added in the *Permit*, *Pickerel*, *Pike*, *Porpoise*, and *Tarpon*.

First group

Displacement:	1,310/1,960 tons.
Dimensions:	283(wl) 301(oa) × 25 × 13 feet.
Machinery:	Two shafts; 16-cylinder Winton type 201A diesel engines (two/shaft)/Elliot electric motors (two/shaft) B.H.P./S.H.P. 4,300/2,085 = 19/8 knots.
Bunkers & radius:	O.F. 373 tons/240-cell Exide battery; ....../... miles @ ../.. knots.
Armament:	One 3-inch/50cal, two ·5-inch A.A. (2 × 1), two ·3-inch A.A. (2 × 1) guns; six 21-inch (four fwd & two aft—sixteen torpedoes) T.T.
Complement:	55.
Diving depth:	250 feet.

Hull No.	Name	Builder	Launched	Fate
SS.172	*Porpoise*	Portsmouth N.Y.	20.6.35	Sold Southern Scrap Material (New Orleans) 14/5/57 & scrapped.
SS.173	*Pike*	,,	12.9.35	Sold A. G. Schoonmaker Co. (New York) 14/1/57 & scrapped.

Machinery contracts: Engined by Winton (diesel engines), and Elliot Motor (electric motors).

Hull No.	Name	Builder	Launched	Fate
SS.174	*Shark* (i)	Electric Boat (Groton)	21.5.35	Lost—cause unknown—east of Menado 11/2/42, or north of Kendari 17/2/42, or east of Kendari 21/2/42.
SS.175	*Tarpon*	,,	12.3.36	Sold Boston Scrap & Metal Co., wrecked in tow 35 m south-south-west Cape Hatteras 26/8/57 en route Baltimore.

Machinery contracts: Engined by Winton (diesel engines), and Elliot Motor (electric motors).

Early war view of the PORPOISE *with W/T mast re-sited at fore end of conning tower, and a 20 mm A.A. gun and GW.RDF added*
[Photograph U.S. Navy

The Porpoise *(above) and the* Permit *(below) with standard war modifications*

War modifications to the PICKEREL *(left) looking aft and the* PERMIT *(above looking forward. Two external T.T. have been added in the bows, the deck gun has been moved to forward of the conning tower, 20 mm A.A. guns have been fitted forward and aft of the conning tower, the W/T mast has been re-sited to forward of the conning tower, and GW.RDF and D/F have been added*

[Photographs U.S. Navy

The PIKE *in February 1944 with standard war modifications*

SS.176	*Perch* (i)	Electric Boat (Groton)	9.5.36	Depth charged I.J.N. destroyers 1–2/3/42 Java Sea and scuttled 3/2/42.
SS.177	*Pickerel* (i)	,,	7.7.36	Depth charged I.J.N. surface vessels north of Honshu 3/4/43.
SS.178	*Permit* (ex-*Pinna*)	,,	5.10.36	Sold A. G. Schoonmaker Co. (New York) 20/6/58 & scrapped.
SS.179	*Plunger*	Portsmouth N.Y.	8.7.36	Sold Bethlehem Steel (Bethlehem) 22/4/57 & scrapped.
SS.180	*Pollack*	,,	15.9.36	Sold Ship-Shape Inc. (Philadelphia) 2/2/47 & scrapped.
SS.181	*Pompano* (i)	Mare Island N.Y. (Vallejo)	11.3.37	Lost—probably mined—east of Honshu 29/8–27/9/43.

Second group

Displacement:	1,315/1,968 tons.
Dimensions:	287(wl) 298(oa) × 25 × 13¾ feet.
Machinery:	As in *first group* except speed 19½/8¼ knots.
Bunkers & *radius:*	O.F. 347 tons/240-cell Exide battery; ..,..../... miles @ ../.. knots.
Armament:	As in first group except one 4-inch/50cal gun.
Complement and *Diving depth:*	As in *first group.*

Third group

Displacement:	1,330 except *Plunger* & *Pollack* 1,335/1,997 tons.
Dimensions:	298(wl) 300½(oa) × 25 × 13¾ feet.
Machinery:	Two shafts; Winton diesel engines (two/shaft)/General Electric electric motors (four/shaft) in *Perch, Pickerel* & *Permit* or Fairbanks Morse diesel engines (two/shaft)/Elliot electric motors (two/shaft) in *Plunger* & *Pollack* or H.O.R. diesel engines (two/shaft)/Allis-Chalmers electric motors (two/shaft) in *Pompano* B.H.P./S.H.P. 4,300/2,336 (*Perch, Pickerel* & *Permit*) or 2,285 (*Plunger, Pollack* & *Pompano*) = 19¼/8¾ knots.
Bunkers & *radius:*	O.F. 371 tons/240-cell Gould battery; ..,..../... miles @ .₂/.. knots.
Armament:	One 4-inch/50cal, two ·5-inch A.A. (2 × 1), four ·3-inch A.A. (2 × 2) guns; six 21-inch (four fwd & two aft—sixteen except *Perch, Pickerel* & *Permit* eighteen torpedoes) T.T.
Complement and *Diving depth:*	As in *first group.*

Machinery contracts: *Perch, Pickerel,* and *Permit* engined by Winton (diesel engines) and General Electric (electric motors); *Plunger* and *Pollack* by Fairbanks Morse and Elliot Motor; and *Pompano* by Hooven Owens Rentschler and Allis-Chalmers.

"Salmon"/"Sargo" classes: First group **SALMON, SEAL, SKIPJACK, SNAPPER, STINGRAY, STURGEON.**
Second group **SARGO, SAURY, SCULPIN, SEADRAGON, SEALION, SEARAVEN, SEAWOLF, SPEARFISH, SQUALUS, SWORDFISH**

To accommodate a slightly higher surfaced speed and a stronger torpedo armament there were small increases in displacement and dimensions with this class; and they were an excellent return for their size, being able to motor far and fast with a useful armament. In comparison their Japanese counterparts of the "I.74" class made 23/8 knots with B.H.P./S.H.P. 9,000/1,800 on 1,420/2,564 tons, had a surfaced radius of about 16,000 miles at 16 knots, and were armed with one 4·7in gun and six 21in T.T. plus eight reloads; from which it is evident that the Imperial Navy was prepared to sacrifice armament for a higher surfaced speed.

An unusual feature of the design was the reversion to composite drive, so that with each pair of diesel engines one powered a generator while the other was coupled to the shaft via gearing. Also driving into each gearbox were two electric motors, and this twin-input arrangement was chosen to restrict the size of the motor so that the armature could be removed through the engine room hatch and it was not necessary to cut the hull. While the composite system operated satisfactorily the last four units—the *Seadragon, Sealion, Searaven,* and *Seawolf*—were fitted with

Hull No.	Name	Builder	Launched	Fate
SS.182	Salmon	Electric Boat (Groton)	12.6.37	Sold .... (.............) 4/4/46 and scrapped.
SS.183	Seal	,,	25.8.37	Sold .... (.............) 8/5/57 and scrapped.
SS.184	Skipjack	,,	23.10.37	Expended as target Bikini 7/46, scuttled 100m. × south-west San Francisco 16/10/48.

geared diesel-electric drive and had a single large electric motor on each shaft, an arrangement that facilitated ship-board repair and maintenance.

All these units first wore the pendant numbers S.1–16 but later adopted the standard hull numbers. The *Squalus* foundered on trials in 1939 and after being salved was placed back in service the following year as the *Sailfish*. During the war the conning tower was modified and reduced in size so that two 20mm A.A. (2 × 1) guns could be mounted.

First group

Displacement:	1,449/2,198 tons.
Dimensions:	....(wl) 308(oa) × 26¼ × 14¼ feet.
Machinery:	Two shafts; H.O.R. (*Salmon, Seal & Skipjack*) or General Motors (*Snapper, Stingray & Sturgeon*) diesel engines (two/shaft) & Elliot electric motors B.H.P./S.H.P. 5,500/3,300 = 21/9 knots.
Bunkers & radius:	O.F. 384 tons/252-cell Gould (*Salmon, Seal & Skipjack*) or Exide (*Snapper, Stingray & Sturgeon*) battery; ..,....,/... miles @ ../.. knots.
Armament:	One 4-inch except *Sturgeon* 3-inch, two ·5-inch A.A. (2 × 1), two ·3-inch A.A. (2 × 1) guns; eight 21-inch (four fwd & four aft—twenty-four torpedoes) T.T.
Complement:	70.
Diving depth:	250 feet.

SS.185	*Snapper*	Portsmouth N.Y.	24.8.37	Sold Interstate Metals (New York) 18/5/48 & scrapped.
SS.186	*Stingray*	,,	6.10.37	Sold Ship-Shape Inc. (Philadelphia) 6/1/47 & scrapped.
SS.187	*Sturgeon*	Mare Island N.Y.	15.3.38	Sold Interstate Metals (New York) 12/6/48 & scrapped.

Machinery contracts: *Salmon, Seal,* and *Skipjack* engined by Hooven, Owens, Rentschler and *Snapper, Stingray,* and *Sturgeon* by General Motors (diesel engines); and by Elliot Motor (electric motors).

Hull No.	Name	Builder	Launched	Fate
SS.188	Sargo	Electric Boat (Groton)	6.6.38	Sold Learner Co. (Oakland) 19/5/47 & scrapped.
SS.189	Saury	,,	20.8.38	Sold Learner Co. (Oakland) 19/5/47 & scrapped.
SS.190	Spearfish	,,	29.10.38	Sold Learner Co. (Oakland) 19/5/47 & scrapped.
SS.191	Sculpin (i)	Portsmouth N.Y.	27.7.38	Depth charged and gunfire I.J.N. destroyer Yamagumo north-east of Truk 19/11/43 and scuttled.
SS.192	Squalus	,,	14.9.38	Foundered on trials off Portsmouth 23/5/39, salved 2/40 and Sailfish (1940); sold .... (............) 18/6/48 and scrapped.
SS.193	Swordfish	Mare Island N.Y. (Vallejo)	1.4.39	Depth charged I.J.N. A/S vessels (or mined?) north of Okinawa 12/1/45.
SS.194	Seadragon	Electric boat (Groton)	21.4.39	Sold Luria Bros. Co. (Philadelphia) 2/7/48 & scrapped.
SS.195	Sealion (i)	,,	25.5.39	Bombed I.J.N. aircraft Cavite 10/12/41 and scuttled 25/12/41.

The STINGRAY *(above) with early war modifications; and the* SNAPPER *(below) with late war modifications: note shape of the conning tower* [Photographs U.S. Navy

Details of war modifications to the SturGEON *showing deck gun mounted forward of the conning tower, 20 mm A.A. guns shipped forward and aft of the conning tower, and the addition of GW.RDF and D/F* [Photograph U.S. Navy

Second group

Displacement:	1,450/2,350 tons.
Dimensions:	....(wl) $310\frac{1}{2}$(oa) × 27 × $13\frac{3}{4}$ feet.
Machinery:	Two shafts; General Motors except *Sargo, Saury, Spearfish & Seadragon* H.O.R. diesel engines (two/shaft) & General Electric electric motors (two/shaft in *Sargo, Saury, Sculpin, Spearfish, Squalus & Swordfish*) B.H.P./S.H.P. 5,500/2,740 = 20/$8\frac{3}{4}$ knots.
Bunkers & radius:	O.F. 428 tons/252-cell Exide battery; ....../... miles @ ../.. knots.
Armament:	As in *first group.*
Complement and *Diving depth:*	As in *first group.*

Hull No.	Name	Builder	Launched	Fate
SS.196	*Searaven*	Portsmouth N.Y.	21.6.39	Expended as target off San Francisco 11/9/48.
SS.197	*Seawolf*	,,	17.8.39	Depth charged in error destroyer escort *Rowell* off Morotai 3/10/44.

Machinery contracts: Engined by General Motors except *Sargo, Saury, Spearfish,* and *Seadragon* by Hooven, Owens, Rentschler (diesel engines); and by General Electric (electric motors).

The STINGRAY *(above) and the* SCULPIN *(below) with standard war modifications*

The SAILFISH *(ex-*SQUALUS—*above) and the* SWORDFISH *(below): note lengthened conning tower of the latter and the* SCULPIN *(left)*
[Photograph U.S. Navy

The TAUTOG *(above) and the* TAMBOR *(below): both mount the deck gun abaft the conning tower, and the latter has a 40 mm. A.A. gun in the after position*

[Photographs U.S. Navy

"Tambor"/"Gar" classes: First group **TAMBOR, TAUTOG, THRESHER, TRITON, TROUT, TUNA.** *Second group* **GAR, GRAMPUS, GRAYBACK, GRAYLING, GRENADIER, GUDGEON**

The design generally followed that of the *Salmon* except that direct drive was re-introduced, and bow fire was increased to six tubes although the number of torpedoes carried remained unaltered.

The diesel engines were arranged in tandem but difficulty was experienced in coupling them together, the after engines experienced more use and wear than the forward units, and while re-charging batteries only half the power was available on one shaft.

War modifications included re-modelling the conning tower so that two 20mm A.A. (2 × 1) guns could be added forward and aft of it, and replacing the 3in by a 5in gun.

Early war view of the TROUT *with the 5-inch deck gun abaft the conning tower*   [Photographs U.S. Navy

Hull No.	Name	Builder	Launched	Fate
SS.198	*Tambor*	Electric Boat (Groton)	20.12.39	Sold Construction Aggregate Corp. (. . . ..) 19/11/59 & scrapped.
SS.199	*Tautog*	,,	27.1.40	Sold Bultena Dock & Dredge (. . . . .) 13/7/60 & scrapped.
SS.200	*Thresher*	,,	27.3.40	Sold . . . . (. . . . .) 18/3/48 & scrapped.
SS.201	*Triton*	Portsmouth N.Y.	25.3.40	Depth charged I.J.N. destroyers north of New Guinea 15/3/43.
SS.202	*Trout*	,,	21.5.40	Depth charged I.J.N. A/S vessels and aircraft south-east of Okinawa 29/2/44
SS.203	*Tuna*	Mare Island N.Y. (Vallejo)	2.10.40	Scuttled as target off San Francisco 25/9/48.
SS.206	*Gar*	Electric Boat (Groton)	7.11.40	Sold Acme Scrap Iron & Metal Co. (. . . . .) 18/11/59 and scrapped.
SS.207	*Grampus* (i)	,,	23.12.40	Depth charged I.J.N. destroyers Blackett Strait 5–6/3/45.
SS.208	*Grayback*	,,	31.1.41	Depth charged I.J.N. A/S vessels and aircraft East China Sea 26/2/44.

SS.209	*Grayling* (i)	Portsmouth N.Y.	4.9.40	Lost—cause unknown—off Luzon 9–12/9/43.
SS.210	*Grenadier* (i)	,,	29.11.40	Depth charged Japanese aircraft north-west of Penang 20/4/43 and scuttled following day.
SS.211	*Gudgeon*	Mare Island N.Y. (Vallejo)	25.1.41	Lost—cause unknown—north of Mariannas 16/4–11/5/44.

Machinery contracts: *Tambor, Tautog, Thresher, Gar, Grampus,* and *Grayback* engined by General Motors and *Triton, Trout, Tuna, Grayling, Grenadier,* and *Gudgeon* by Fairbanks Morse (diesel engines); and by General Electric (electric motors).

Early war modifications to the GAR *included the addition of light A.A. guns and GW.RDF*   [Photograph U.S. Navy

By the close of the war the GROUPER *shipped 40 mm. A.A. guns forward and aft of the conning tower, and the deck gun has been moved forward*

Displacement:	1,475/2,370 tons.
Dimensions:	....(wl) 307¾(oa) × 27¼ × 13¾ feet.
Machinery:	Two shafts; General Motors (in *Tambor, Tautog, Thresher, Gar, Grampus & Grayback*) or Fairbanks Morse (in *Triton, Trout, Tuna, Grayling, Grenadier & Gudgeon*) diesel engines (two/shaft) & General Electric electric motors B.H.P./S.H.P. 5,400/2,740 = 20/8¾ knots.
Bunkers & radius:	O.F. *first group* 374 tons, *second group* 385 tons/252-cell Exide battery; ....../... miles @ ../.. knots.
Armament:	One 3-inch/50cal, two ·5-inch A.A. (2 × 1), two ·3-inch A.A. (2 × 1) guns; ten 21-inch (six fwd & four aft—twenty-four torpedoes) T.T.
Complement:	80–85.
Diving depth:	250 feet.

Although principally used for training standard war modifications were applied to the medium-sized **MARLIN**

[Photograph U.S. Navy

It was never plainly evident what prompted the construction of these medium-sized submarines while the United States Navy had a large reserve of older boats to draw on of similar size, and for which they had little operational use. They were always referred to as experimental units, and were used for training throughout the war. Both had direct drive, but while the *Marlin's* machinery drove through reduction gearing that for the *Mackerel* was directly coupled; and only the former was modified during the war to ship two 20mm A.A. (2 × 1) guns forward and aft of the conning tower.

Displacement:	825/1,179 tons.
Dimensions:	....(pp) 239(oa) × 21¾ × 12 feet.
Machinery:	Two shafts; .... diesel engines & Electro Dynamic electric motors (*Mackerel*) or ALCO diesel engines & General Electric electric motors (*Marlin*) B.H.P./S.H.P. 3,360 (*Mackerel*) or 3,400 (*Marlin*)/1,500 = 16/9 knots.
Bunkers & radius:	O.F. 116 tons/120-cell Exide battery; .,..../... miles @ ../.. knots.
Armament:	One 3-inch/50cal, two ·5-inch A.A. (2 × 1), two ·3-inch A.A. (2 × 1) guns; six 21-inch (four fwd & two aft—twelve torpedoes) T.T.
Complement:	38.
Diving depth:	250 feet.

SS.204	*Mackerel*	Electric Boat (Groton)	28.9.40	Sold North American Smelting Co. (Philadelphia) 24/4/47 and scrapped.
SS.205	*Marlin*	Portsmouth N.Y.	29.1.41	Sold Boston Metals Co. (Baltimore) 29/3/46 and scrapped.

Machinery contracts: *Mackerel* engined by builders, and *Marlin* by American Locomotive Co. (diesel engines); and *Mackerel* by Electro Dynamics, and *Marlin* by General Electric (electric motors).

"Gato" class: **ALBACORE, AMBERJACK, ANGLER, BARB, BASHAW, BLACKFISH, BLUEFISH, BLUE-GILL, BONEFISH, BREAM, CAVALLA, CERO, COBIA, COD, CORVINA, CROAKER, DACE, DARTER, DORADO, DRUM, FINBACK, FLASHER, FLIER, FLOUNDER, FLYING FISH, GABILAN, GATO, GREEN-LING, GROUPER, GROWLER, GRUNION, GUARDFISH, GUNNEL, GURNARD, HADDO, HADDOCK, HAKE, HALIBUT, HARDER, HERRING, HOE, JACK, KINGFISH, LAPON, MINGO, MUSKALLUNGE, PADDLE, PARGO, PETO, POGY, POMPON, PUFFER, RASHER, RATON, RAY, REDFIN, ROBALO, ROCK, RUNNER, SAWFISH, SCAMP, SCORPION, SHAD, SILVERSIDES, SNOOK, STEELHEAD, SUN-FISH, TINOSA, TRIGGER, TULLIBEE, TUNNY, WAHOO, WHALE**

The accumulated experience of all classes from the *Porpoise* went into this final pre-war design, of which over two-hundred were ultimately authorised. To reduce the volume of the engine room it was divided into two compartments; and as a result the *Gato* was 4ft longer than, but otherwise closely similar to, the *Tambor*. Propulsion was by geared diesel-electric drive, with four diesel generators supplying power to two electric motors coupled to the shafts through reduction gearing.

Following the outbreak of hostilities the *Gato* was adopted as the standard design to put into war production—for which its all-welded construction made it eminently suitable—and with only small modification construction continued throughout the war years. Such alterations as occurred were mainly internal to accommodate new and/or improved equipment. From the *Balao* (SS.285) the hull was strengthened to increase the diving depth; and from the *Clamagore* (SS.343) the electric motors were directly coupled to the shafts to eliminate the noise associated with reduction gearing and to secure quiet operation when running submerged. Habitability was of a very high standard (for submarines) with air-conditioned accommodation and separate sleeping and eating quarters; and paid dividends in keeping the crew healthy—and so alert—during long patrols invariably carried out under arduous climatic conditions.

The original provision for the "Gato" class was to mount a 3in gun abaft the conning tower, and while some of the earlier units were so completed the general trend was:
(a) to remount the gun forward of the conning tower and later replace it with a 4in (in a few units) or 5in gun;
(b) ship a 20mm A.A. gun on the after end of the conning tower; and
(c) modify the conning tower structure so that an additional 20mm A.A. gun could be shipped forward,
and most of the later boats were completed with a gun armament of one 5in/25cal A.A. and two 20mm A.A. (2 × 1) in the first instance.

Hull No.	Name	Builder	Launched	Fate
SS.212	*Gato*	Electric Boat (Groton)	21.8.41	Sold Northern Metals Co. (Philadelphia) 25/7/60 and scrapped.
SS.213	*Greenling*	,,	20.9.41	Sold Minichiello Bros. (Chelsea, Mass.) 16/6/60 and scrapped.
SS.214	*Grouper*	,,	27.10.41	SSK.214 (1951), AGSS.214 (1958); sold Lancet Inc. (Brookline) 11/8/70 & scrapped.
SS.215	*Growler*	,,	2.11.41•	Lost—cause unknown—South China Sea 8/11/44.
SS.216	*Grunion*	,,	22.12.41	Lost—cause unknown—off Kiska . . /7/42.
SS.217	*Guardfish*	,,	20.1.42	Expended as target off New London 10/10/61.
SS.218	*Albacore*	,,	17.2.42	Mined off Hakodate 7/11/44.
SS.219	*Amberjack* (i)	,,	6.3.42	Depth charged I.J.N. torpedo boat *Hiyodori*, sub-chaser *No. 18* and aircraft off New Britain 16/2/43.
SS.220	*Barb*	,,	2.4.42	Italian Navy *Enrico Tazzoli* (1955).
SS.221	*Blackfish*	,,	18.8.42	Stricken . . / . . /59 and scrapped.

The AMBERJACK *as completed on 9 May 1942 with original large conning tower* [Photograph U.S. Navy]

With the "Balao" class most boats were completed with the 5in gun forward of the conning tower and two 20mm A.A. (2 × 1) guns, but a later modification was to ship a 40mm A.A. in place of the forward 20mm A.A. gun, and those units not completed to this arrangement were subsequently altered to it.

"Gato" class

Displacement:	1,526/2,424 except *SS.228–235* & *275–280* 2,410 tons.
Dimensions:	307(wl) 311¾(oa) × 27¼ × 15¼ feet.
Machinery:	Two shafts; 10-cylinder Fairbanks Morse type 38D–1/8 (in *SS.228–239* & *275–284*) or 16-cylinder General Motors type 278A (in *SS.212–227, 240–252* & *265–274*) or H.O.R. (in *SS.253–264*) diesel engines (two/shaft)/General Electric (in *SS.212–227, 236–256* & *265–284*) or Elliot Motor (in *SS.228–235*) or Allis-Chalmers (in *SS.257–264*) electric motors B.H.P./S.H.P. 5,400/2,740 = 20¼/8¾ knots.
Bunkers & radius:	O.F. 389 except *SS.228–235* & *275–280* 378 and *SS.236–239, 265–274* & *281–284* 464 tons/252-cell Exide except *SS.261, 275–278* & *280* Gould battery; ....../... miles @ ../.. knots.
Armament:	One 3-inch/50cal A.A., two ·5-inch A.A. (2 × 1), two ·3-inch A.A. (2 × 1) guns; ten 21-inch (six forward & four aft—twenty-four torpedoes) T.T.
Complement:	80–85.
Diving depth:	300 feet.

Hull No.	Name	Builder	Launched	Fate
SS.222	*Bluefish*	,,	21.2.43	Sold Richard Storkorb (. . . . .) 17/11/59 & scrapped.
SS.223	*Bonefish*	,,	7.3.43	Depth charged I.J.N. A/S vessels off Toyama Wan 18/6/45.
SS.224	*Cod*	,,	21.3.43	AGSS.224 (1962), IXSS.224 (1971); stricken 15/12/71.
SS.225	*Cero*	,,	4.4.43	AGSS.225 (1962); stricken 30/6/67 and hulked as memorial St. Louis (Ill.).
SS.226	*Corvina*	,,	9.5.43	Torpedoed I.J.N. submarine *I.176* south of Truk 16/11/43.
SS.227	*Darter*	,,	6.6.43	Wrecked Bombat Strait 24/10/44.
SS.228	*Drum*	Portsmouth N.Y.	12.5.41	AGSS.228 (1962); stricken 30/6/68 & hulked as relic Mobile.
SS.229	*Flying Fish*	,,	4.7.41	AGSS.229 (1950); sold North American Salvage Co. (. . . . .) 1/5/59 & scrapped.
SS.230	*Finback*	,,	25.8.41	Sold Northern Metals (Philadelphia) . ./8/59 & scrapped.

In the SILVERSIDES *(above & below) a 3-inch A.A. gun has replaced the 5-inch deck gun mounted in the earlier units*

SS.231	*Haddock*	Portsmouth N.Y.	20.10.41	Sold J. Checkoway (. . . . .) 23/8/60 and scrapped.
SS.232	*Halibut*	,,	3.12.41	Depth charged Japanese aircraft Luzon Strait 14/1/44 and written-off as constructive total loss; sold Quaker Shyd. & Machy. Co. (Camden) 10/1/47 and scrapped.
SS.233	*Herring*	,,	15.1.42	Gunfire Japanese shore battery Point Tagan (Kuriles) 1/6/44.
SS.234	*Kingfish*	,,	2.3.42	Sold A. Heller (. . . . .) 6/10/60 and scrapped.

The SHAD *has a 5-inch deck gun forward of the conning tower which has been modified to ship a 20 mm. A.A. gun on its after end*   [Photograph U.S. Navy

In the TRIGGER *an additional 20 mm. A.A. gun has been mounted forward of the conning tower*   [Photograph U.S. Navy]

SS.235	*Shad*	Portsmouth N.Y.	15.4.42	Sold Luria Bros. Inc. (Philadelphia) 21/6/60 & scrapped.
SS.236	*Silversides*	Mare Island N.Y. (Vallejo)	26.8.41	AGSS.236 (1962); stricken 30/6/69 & scrapped.
SS.237	*Trigger*	,,	22.10.41	Depth charged I.J.N. A/S vessels & aircraft Nansei Shoto Archipelago 28/3/45.
SS.238	*Wahoo* (i)	,,	14.2.42	Bombed Japanese aircraft La Perouse Strait 12/10/43.

Hull No.	Name	Builder	Launched	Fate
SS.239	*Whale*	Mare Island N.Y. (Vallejo)	14.3.42	Sold Southern Scrap Metals (New Orleans) 29/9/60 & scrapped.
SS.240	*Angler*	Electric Boat (Groton)	4.7.43	SSK.240 (1953), SS.240 (1959), AGSS.240 (1963), IXSS.240 (1971); stricken 15/12/71.
SS.241	*Bashaw*	,,	25.7.43	SSK.241 (1953), SS.241 (1959), AGSS.241 (1962); stricken 13/9/69 & expended as target.
SS.242	*Bluegill*	,,	8.8.43	SSK.242 (1953), SS.242 (1959), AGSS.242 (1962); scuttled for training 2/12/70.
SS.243	*Bream*	,,	17.10.43	SSK.243 (1953), SS.243 (1959), AGSS.243 (1965); expended as target off . . . . 8/11/69.
SS.244	*Cavalla*	,,	14.11.43	SSK.244 (1953), SS.244 (1959), AGSS.244 (1963); stricken 30/12/69 & hulked as memorial Galveston.
SS.245	*Cobia*	,,	28.11.43	AGSS.245 (1962); stricken 1/7/70 & hulked as memorial Manitowoc.
SS.246	*Croaker*	,,	19.12.43	SSK.246 (1953), SS.246 (1959), AGSS.246 (1967), IXSS.246 (1971); stricken 20/12/71.

The CAVALLA in surface trim with standard arrangement of deck gun forward and light A.A. guns forward and aft of the conning tower [Photograph U.S. Navy

Hull No.	Name	Builder	Launched	Fate
SS.247	*Dace*	Electric Boat (Groton)	25.4.43	Italian Navy *Leonardo da Vinci* (1955).
SS.248	*Dorado* (i)	,,	23.5.43	Bombed in error U.S.N. aircraft Canal Zone area 12/10/43.
SS.249	*Flasher*	,,	20.6.43	Sold Intercontinental Eng. & Mfg. Co. (Roebling) . . /6/63 & scrapped.
SS.250	*Flier*	,,	11.7.43	Lost—probably mined—Balabac Strait 13/8/44.
SS.251	*Flounder*	,,	22.8.43	Sold Western Contracting Corp. (. . . . . .) 22/12/59 & scrapped.
SS.252	*Gabilan*	,,	19.9.43	Sold Ship Supply Co. (. . . . .) 15/12/59 & scrapped.
SS.253	*Gunnel*	,,	17.5.42	Sold Luria Bros. Inc. (Philadelphia) . . /8/59 & scrapped.
SS.254	*Gurnard*	,,	1.6.42	Sold National Steel Corp. (Terminal Island) 26/9/61 & scrapped.
SS.255	*Haddo*	,,	21.6.42	Sold Luria Bros. Inc. (Philadelphia) 30/4/59 & scrapped.

The HARDER *(above)* and the FLASHER *(below)*

Hull No.	Name	Builder	Launched	Fate
SS.256	*Hake*	Electric Boat (Groton)	17.7.42	AGSS.256 (1962); stricken 1/3/67 & hulked for salvage training.
SS.257	*Harder*	,,	19.8.42	Depth charged I.J.N. minesweeper off Point Caiman 24/8/44.
SS.258	*Hoe*	,,	17.9.42	Sold Lansett Inc. (Boston) 23/8/60 & scrapped.
SS.259	*Jack*	,,	16.10.42	R.H.N. *Amfitriti* (1958).
SS.260	*Lapon*	,,	27.10.42	R.H.N. *Poseidon* (1957).
SS.261	*Mingo*	,,	30.11.42	J.M.S.D.F. *Kuroshio* (1955); returned U.S.N. 20/2/71 & scrapped Japan.
SS.262	*Muskallunge*	,,	13.12.42	Brazilian Navy *Humaita* (1957).
SS.263	*Paddle*	,,	30.12.42	Brazilian Navy *Riachuelo* (1957)
SS.264	*Pargo*	,,	24.1.43	Sold Houston Armature Works (Houston) 17/4/61 & scrapped.
SS.265	*Peto*	Manitowoc Sbdg.	30.4.42	Sold Commercial Metals (. . . . .) 25/11/60 & scrapped.

A 40 mm. A.A. has replaced the light A.A. gun forward in the RAY *(above) while the deck gun is mounted abaft the conning tower. This arrangement is transposed in the* JACK *(below) which has the deck gun forward and the 40 mm. A.A. gun aft*

[Photographs U.S. Navy

Hull No.	Name	Builder	Launched	Fate
SS.266	*Pogy*	Manitowoc Sbdg.	22.6.42	Sold . . . . (. . . . .) 1/5/59 & scrapped.
SS.267	*Pompon*	,,	15.8.42	SSR.267 (1951); sold Commercial Metals (. . . . .) 25/11/60 & scrapped.
SS.268	*Puffer*	,,	22.11.42	Sold Zidell Explorations Inc. (Portland) 4/11/60 & scrapped.
SS.269	*Rasher*	,,	20.12.42	SSR.269 (1951), SS.269 (1959); AGSS.269 (1960), IXSS.269 (1971); stricken 20/12/71.
SS.270	*Raton*	,,	24.1.43	AGSS.270 (1960); expended as target off . . . . 12/9/69.
SS.271	*Ray*	,,	28.2.43	SSR.271 (1951); stricken ../../60 & scrapped.
SS.272	*Redfin*	,,	4.4.43	SSR.272 (1951), SS.272 (1959), AGSS.272 (1963); sold North American Smelting (Wilmington) ../3/71 & scrapped.
SS.273	*Robalo*	,,	9.5.43	Lost—probably mined—off west coast of Palawan 26/7/44.

OFFICIAL PHOTOGRAPH
NOT TO BE RELEASED FOR PUBLICATION
Photo No. 61 Taken 4-30-1942
View: Launching
Manitowoc Shipbuilding Company
Manitowoc, Wisconsin.

Hull No.	Name	Builder	Launched	Fate
SS.274	*Rock*	Manitowoc Sbdg.	20.6.43	SSR.274 (1951), SS.274 (1959), AGSS.274 (1960); stricken 13/9/69 & expended as target.
SS.275	*Runner* (i)	Portsmouth N.Y.	30.5.42	Lost—probably mined—south of Hokkaido 28/5–7/6/43.
SS.276	*Sawfish*	,,	23.6.42	Sold National Metal & Steel (Terminal Island) 14/11/60 & scrapped.
SS.277	*Scamp*	,,	20.7.42	Lost—cause unknown—south-east of Honshu 9–16/11/44.
SS.278	*Scorpion*	,,	20.7.42	Lost—probably mined—East China Sea 6–16/2/44.
SS.279	*Snook*	,,	15.8.42	Lost—unknown cause—south-east of Hainan 8–20/4/45.
SS.280	*Steelhead*	,,	11.9.42	Sold National Metal & Steel (Terminal Island) 29/6/61 & scrapped.
SS.281	*Sunfish*	Mare Island N.Y. (Vallejo)	2.5.42	Sold Learner Co. (Oakland) 29/11/60 & scrapped.

The ROCK *as completed* [Photograph U.S. Navy

Hull No.	Name	Builder	Launched	Fate
SS.282	*Tunny*	Mare Island N.Y. (Vallejo)	30.6.42	SSG.282 (1951), APSS.282 (1960), LPSS. 282 (1969); expended as target off Southern California 19/6/69.
SS.283	*Tinosa*	,,	7.10.42	Stricken ../../59 & hulked for salvage training; foundered off Pearl Harbour ../../61.
SS.284	*Tullibee*	,,	11.11.42	Self-torpedoed north of Palau 26/3/44.

Machinery contracts: Engined by General Motors except *SS.228–239* and *275–284* by Fairbanks Morse, and *SS.253–264* by Hooven, Owens, Rentschler (diesel engines); and by General Electric except *SS.228–235* by Elliot Motor, and *SS.257–264* by Allis-Chalmers (electric motors).

"Balao" class: **APAGON, ARCHERFISH, ASPRO, ATULE, BALAO, BANG, BARBEL, BARBERO, BATFISH, BAYA, BECUNA, BERGALL, BESUGO, BILLFISH, BLACKFIN, BLENNY, BLOWER, BLUEBACK, BOARFISH, BOWFIN, BRILL, BUGARA, BULLHEAD, BUMPER, BURRFISH, CABEZON, CABRILLA, CAIMAN, CAPELIN, CAPITAINE, CARBONERO, CARP, CATFISH, CHARR, CHIVO, CHOPPER, CHUB, CISCO, CLAMAGORE, COBBLER, COCHINO, CORPORAL, CREVALLE, CUSK, DENTUDA, DEVILFISH, DIODON, DOGFISH, DRAGONET, DUGONG, EEL, ESPADA, ENTEMEDOR, ESCOLAR, GARLOPA, GARRUPA, GOLDRING, GOLET, GREENFISH, GUAVINA, GUITARRO, HACKLEBACK, HALFBEAK, HAMMERHEAD, HARDHEAD, HAWKBILL, ICEFISH, JALLAO, JAWFISH, KETE, KRAKEN, LAGARTO, LAMPREY, LANCETFISH, LING, LIONFISH, LIZARDFISH, LOGGERHEAD, MACABI, MANTA, MAPIRO, MENHADEN, MERO, MORAY, NEEDLEFISH, NERKA, ONO, PAMPANITO, PARCHE, PERCH, PICUDA, PILOTFISH, PINTADO, PIPEFISH, PIPER, PIRANHA, PLAICE, POMFRET, QUEENFISH, RAZORBACK, REDFISH, RONCADOR, RONQUIL, SABALO, SABLEFISH, SANDLANCE, SCABBARDFISH, SEA DEVIL, SEA DOG, SEA FOX, SEA OWL, SEA POACHER, SEA ROBIN, SEAHORSE, SEALION, SEGUNDO, SENNET, SHARK, SKATE, SPADEFISH, SPIKEFISH, SPOT, SPRINGER, STERLET, STICKLEBACK, TANG, THREADFIN, TILEFISH, TIRU, TREPANG**

Modified arrangement of the CREVALLE *with a 40 mm. A.A. gun abaft the conning tower and the deck gun mounted aft*
[Photograph U.S. Navy

The BARBERO *as completed with the deck gun forward and 20 mm. A.A. guns forward and aft of the conning tower*

[Photograph U.S. Navy

"Balao" class

Displacement:	1,526/2,424 except *SS.285–291* 2,414 and *SS.308–312* & *381–404* 2,391 and *SS.405–410* 2,401 tons.
Dimensions:	307(wl) 311¾(oa) × 27¼ × 15¼ feet.
Machinery:	Two shafts; 16-cylinder General Motors type 278A except *SS.292–312* & *381–416* 10-cylinder Fairbanks Morse type 38D–1/8 diesel engines (two/shaft)/General Electric except *SS.292–312* & *381–416* Elliot Motor electric motors B.H.P./S.H.P. 5,400/2,740 = 20¼/8¾ knots.
Bunkers & *radius:*	O.F. 472 except *SS.285–291,298, 299, 308–312* 378; *SS.292–297, 300–307, 361–364, 381–404* & *411–416* 464 tons/252-cell Exide (in *SS.285–291, 299, 304–311, 313–360, 365, 366, 370–376* & *411–416*) or Gould (in *SS.292–298, 300–303, 312, 361–364, 367–369, 377–380* & *410*) battery; ..,../... miles @ ../.. knots.
Armament:	One 5-inch/25cal except *SS.285–291* 4-inch/50cal and *SS.361–364* 3-inch/50 cal A.A. gun, one 40mm A.A. (not in *SS.361–364*), one 20mm A.A. (in *SS.313–360* & *365–416* only), two ·5-inch except *SS.361–364* ·3-inch A.A. (2 × 1) guns; ten 21-inch (six fwd & four aft—twenty-four torpedoes) T.T.
Complement:	80–85.
Diving depth:	400 except *SS.361–364* 300 feet.

Hull No.	Name	Builder	Launched	Fate
SS.285	Balao	Portsmouth N.Y.	27.10.42	AGSS.285 (1960); expended as target off ..../../64.
SS.286	Billfish	,,	12.11.42	AGSS.286 (1962); sold Eckhardt GmbH (Hamburg) ../1/71 & scrapped.
SS.287	Bowfin	,,	7.12.42	AGSS.287 (1962), IXSS.287 (1971); stricken 1/12/71.
SS.288	Cabrilla	,,	24.12.42	AGSS.288 (1962); sold Southern Scrap Material (New Orleans) ../6/72 and scrapped.
SS.289	Capelin	,,	20.1.43	Lost—cause unknown—Celebes Sea 2–6/12/43.
SS.290	Cisco	,,	24.12.42	Bombed Japanese aircraft and depth charged surface vessels west of Mindanao 28/9/43.
SS.291	Crevalle	,,	22.2.43	AGSS.291 (1961); sold Eckhardt GmbH (Hamburg) ../1/71 & scrapped.
SS.292	Devilfish	Cramp Sbdg. (Philadelphia)	30.5.43	AGSS.292 (1962); expended as target off .... 14/8/68.

The BLACKFIN *(above) had the deck gun abaft the conning tower; while the* BLUEBACK *(below) had 5-inch A.A. deck guns forward and aft, together with two 40 mm. A.A. guns, when fitted as a radar picket*   [Photographs U.S. Navy

Hull No.	Name	Builder	Launched	Fate
SS.293	*Dragonet*	Cramp Sbdg. (Philadelphia)	18.4.43	Expended as target Chesapeake Bay 17/9/61.
SS.294	*Escolar*	,,	18.4.43	Lost—cause unknown—east of Kyushu 17/10/44.
SS.295	*Hackleback*	,,	30.5.43	AGSS.295 (1962); sold Ziddell Explorations Inc. (Portland) 4/12/68 and scrapped.
SS.296	*Lancetfish*	,,	15.8.43	Completed Boston N.Y.; foundered Boston 15/3/45, salved 23/3/45 & paid-off, sold Yale Waste Co. (. . . . .) 27/8/59 and scrapped.
SS.297	*Ling*	,,	15.8.43	Completed Boston N.Y., AGSS.297(1960), IXSS.297 (1971): stricken 1/12/71.
SS.298	*Lionfish*	,,	7.11.43	Completed Portsmouth N.Y., AGSS.298 (1960), IXSS.298(1971): stricken 20/12/71.
SS.299	*Manta*	,,	7.11.43	AGSS.299 (1960); expended as target off Virginia Capes 16/7/69.
SS.300	*Moray*	,,	14.5.44	AGSS.300 (1962); expended as target off Southern California 18/6/70.
SS.301	*Roncador*	,,	14.5.44	AGSS.301 (1962), IXSS.301 (1971); stricken 1/12/71, disposal undetermined.

Owing to its location Manitowoc Shipbuilding has to launch its vessels broadside on, as illustrated by the GUAVINA *on 29 August 1943*
[Photograph U.S. Navy

Hull No.	Name	Builder	Launched	Fate
SS.302	*Sabalo*	Cramp Sbdg. (Philadelphia)	4.6.44	Stricken 1/7/71, disposal undetermined.
SS.303	*Sablefish*	,,	4.6.44	AGSS.303 (1962); sold Union Minerals & Alloy (New York) 29/7/71 & scrapped.
SS.304	*Seahorse*	Mare Island N.Y. (Vallejo)	9.1.43	AGSS.304 (1962); sold Zidell Explorations (Portland) 4/12/68 and scrapped.
SS.305	*Skate*	,,	4.3.43	Scuttled Bikini 16/10/48.
SS.306	*Tang*	,,	17.8.43	Self-torpedoed north-west of Formosa 24/10/44.
SS.307	*Tilefish*	,,	25.10.43	Venezuelan Navy *Carite* (1960).
SS.308	*Apagon* (ex-*Abadejo*)	Portsmouth N.Y.	10.3.43	Expended Bikini 25/7/46.
SS.309	*Aspro* (ex-*Acedia*)	,,	7.4.43	AGSS.309 (1960); expended as target off ..../../63.
SS.310	*Batfish* (ex-*Acoupa*)	,,	5.5.43	AGSS.310 (1962); stricken 1/11/69 & hulked as memorial Muskogee.
SS.311	*Archerfish*	,,	28.5.43	AGSS.311 (1960); expended as target off .... 16/10/68.

The HAWKBILL *(above) has a 5-inch/25-cal. aft while the* HARHEAD *(below) has a 5-inch/51-cal. forward*

Hull No.	Name	Builder	Launched	Fate
SS.312	*Burrfish* (ex-*Arnillo*)	Portsmouth N.Y.	18.6.43	SSR.312 (1948), SS.312 (1961), R.C.N. *Grilse* (1961–69); stricken 31/7/69 & expended as target.
SS.313	*Perch* (ii)	Electric Boat (Groton)	12.9.43	APSS.313 (1948), LPSS.313 (1970), IXSS. 313 (1971); stricken 1/12/71.
SS.314	*Shark* (ii)	,,	17.10.43	Depth charged I.J.N. A/S vessels southwest of Formosa 24/10/44.
SS.315	*Sealion* (ii)	,,	31.10.43	APSS.315 (1948), LPSS.315 (1969).
SS.316	*Barbel*	,,	14.11.43	Bombed Japanese aircraft south-west Palawan Island 4/2/45.
SS.317	*Barbero*	,,	12.12.43	ASSA.317 (1948), SSG.317 (1955); stricken 1/7/64 and expended as target.
SS.318	*Baya*	,,	2.1.44	AGSS.318 (1949).
SS.319	*Becuna*	,,	30.1.44	AGSS.319 (1969), SS.319 (1971).
SS.320	*Bergall*	,,	16.2.44	Turkish Navy *Turgot Reis* (1958).
SS.321	*Besugo*	,,	27.2.44	AGSS.321 (1962); Italian Navy *Francesco Morosini* (1966).

Both the LIZARDFISH *(above) and the* LOGGERHEAD *(below) had the 5-icn/25-cal. deck gun aft, and a 40 mm. A.A. gun forward of the conning tower* [Photographs U.S. Navy

SS.322	*Blackfin*	Electric Boat (Groton)	12.3.44	R.H.N. (1972).
SS.323	*Caiman* (ex-*Blanquillo*)	,,	30.3.44	Stricken 30/6/72.
SS.324	*Blenny*	,,	9.4.44	AGSS.324 (1969), SS.324 (1971).
SS.325	*Blower*	,,	23.4.44	Turkish Navy *Dumlupinar* (1950); foundered Dardenelles 4/4/53.
SS.326	*Blueback*	,,	7.5.44	Turkish Navy *Ikinci Inonu* (1948).
SS.327	*Boarfish*	,,	21.5.44	Turkish Navy *Sakarya* (1948).

The PILOTFISH *had a 40 mm. A.A. gun forward, and a 20 mm. A.A. and the deck gun aft*   [Photograph U.S. Navy

As completed the SPIKEFISH *had light A.A. guns forward and aft of the conning tower, and the deck gun aft*

SS.328	Charr (ex-Bocaccio)	Electric Boat (Groton)	28.5.44	AGSS.328 (1966), IXSS.328 (1971); stricken 20/12/71.
SS.329	Chub (ex-Chubb, ex-Bonaci)	,,	18.6.44	Turkish Navy Gur (1948).
SS.330	Brill	,,	25.6.44	Turkish Navy Birinci Inonu (1948).
SS.331	Bugara	,,	2.7.44	AGSS.331 (1969); accidentally lost off Cape Flattery 1/6/71.

Hull No.	Name	Builder	Launched	Fate
SS.332	Bullhead	Electric Boat (Groton)	16.7.44	Depth charged Japanese Army aircraft south of Bali 6/8/45.
SS.333	Bumper	,,	6.8.44	Turkish Navy Canakkale (1950).
SS.334	Cabezon	,,	27.8.44	AGSS.334 (1962); sold Zidell Explorations (Portland) 28/12/71 & scrapped.
SS.335	Dentuda (ex-Capidoli)	,,	10.9.44	AGSS.335 (1962); sold Zidell Explorations (Portland) 20/1/69 & scrapped.
SS.336	Capitaine	,,	1.10.44	AGSS.336 (1960); Italian Navy Alfredo Cappellini (1966).
SS.337	Carbonero	,,	19.10.44	SSG.337 (1952), SS.337 (1957), AGSS.337 (1969); stricken 1/12/70, disposal undetermined.
SS.338	Carp	,,	12.11.44	AGSS.338 (1968). IXSS.338 (1971); stricken 20/12/71.
SS.339	Catfish	,,	19.11.44	Argentinian Navy Santa Fe (1971).
SS.340	Entemedor (ex-Chickwick)	,,	17.12.44	

Aerial view of the GUITARRO showing hull form, 40 mm A.A. guns forward and aft of the conning tower, and 5in A.A. deck gun mounted on the after deck

[Photograph U.S. Navy

Hull No.	Name	Builder	Launched	Fate
SS.341	*Chivo*	Electric Boat (Groton)	14.1.45	Argentinian Navy *Santiago del Estero* (1971).
SS.342	*Chopper*	,,	4.2.45	AGSS.342 (1969), IXSS.342 (1971); stricken 1/10/71.
SS.343	*Clamagore*	,,	25.2.45	
SS.344	*Cobbler*	,,	1.4.45	
SS.345	*Cochino*	,,	20.4.45	Foundered off north coast of Norway 26/8/49.
SS.346	*Corporal*	,,	10.6.45	
SS.347	*Cubera*	,,	17.6.45	Venezuelan *Tiberon* (1972).
SS.348	*Cusk*	,,	28.7.45	SSG.348 (1948), SS.348 (1954), AGSS.348 (19..); stricken 24/9/69, disposal undetermined.
SS.349	*Diodon*	,,	10.9.45	Sold Nicolai Joffe Corp. (Beverly Hills) ../6/72 and scrapped.
SS.350	*Dogfish*	,,	27.10.45	

Hull No.	Name	Builder	Launched	Fate
SS.351	*Greenfish* (ex-*Doncella*)	Electric Boat (Groton)	21.12.45	
SS.352	*Halfbeak* (ex-*Dory*)	,,	19.2.46	Stricken 1/7/71, disposal undetermined.
SS.353	*Dugong*	,,	—	Cancelled 23/10/44.
SS.354	*Eel*	,,	—	Cancelled 23/10/44.
SS.355	*Espada*	,,	—	Cancelled 23/10/44.
SS.356	*Jawfish* (ex-*Fanegal*)	,,	—	Cancelled 29/7/44.
SS.357	*Ono* (ex-*Friar*)	,,	—	Cancelled 29/7/44.
SS.358	*Garlopa*	,,	—	Cancelled 29/7/44.
SS.359	*Garrupa*	,,	—	Cancelled 29/7/44.
SS.360	*Goldring*	,,	—	Cancelled 29/7/44.

Hull No.	Name	Builder	Launched	Fate
SS.361	*Golet*	Manitowoc Sbdg.	1.8.43	Depth charged I.J.N. A/S vessels north of Honshu 14/6/44.
SS.362	*Guavina*	,,	29.8.43	SSO.362 (1948), AGSS.362 (1952); expended as target 90m × east Cape Henry 14/11/67.
SS.363	*Guitarro*	,,	26.9.43	Turkish Navy *Preveze* (1954); returned U.S.N. 1/1/72 & scrapped Turkey.
SS.364	*Hammerhead*	,,	24.10.43	Turkish Navy *Cerbe* (1954); returned U.S.N. 1/1/72 & scrapped Turkey.
SS.365	*Hardhead*	,,	12.12.43	
SS.366	*Hawkbill*	,,	9.1.44	R.Neth.N. *Zeeleeuw* (1954); returned U.S.N. 24/11/70 and scrapped Netherlands.
SS.367	*Icefish*	,,	20.2.44	R.Neth.N. *Walrus* (1953); returned U.S.N. 15/7/71 and scrapped Netherlands.
SS.368	*Jallao*	,,	12.3.44	
SS.369	*Kete*	,,	9.4.44	Lost—probably torpedoed I.J.N. submarine—south of Kyushu 20–31/3/45.

Hull No.	Name	Builder	Launched	Fate
SS.370	Kraken	Electric Boat (Groton)	30.4.44	Spanish Navy *Almirante Garcia de los Reyes* (1958).
SS.371	Lagarto	,,	28.5.44	Depth charged I.J.N. minelayer *Hatsutaka* Gulf of Siam 3/5/45.
SS.372	Lamprey	,,	18.6.44	Argentinian Navy *Santa Fe* (1960); cannibalised for spares 1971 and scrapped.
SS.373	Lizardfish	,,	16.7.44	Italian Navy *Evangelista Torricelli* (ex-*Luigi Torelli*) (1960).
SS.374	Loggerhead	,,	13.8.44	AGSS.374 (1962); sold Zidell Explorations Inc. (Portland) . ./8/69 & scrapped.
SS.375	Macabi	,,	19.9.44	Argentinian Navy *Santiago del Estero* (1960); cannibalised for spares 1971 and scrapped.
SS.376	Mapiro	,,	9.11.44	Turkish Navy *Piri Reis* (1960).
SS.377	Menhaden	,,	20.12.44	Spanish Navy .... (1971).
SS.378	Mero	,,	17.1.45	Turkish Navy *Hizir Reis* (1960).

Hull No.	Name	Builder	Launched	Fate
SS.379	*Needlefish* (i)	Electric Boat (Groton)	—	Cancelled 29/7/44.
SS.380	*Nerka*	,,	—	Cancelled 29/7/44.
SS.381	*Sand Lance* (ex-*Ojanca*, ex-*Orca*)	Portsmouth N.Y.	25.6.43	Brazilian *Rio Grande do Sul* (1963).
SS.382	*Picuda* (ex-*Obispo*)	,,	12.7.43	
SS.383	*Pampanito*	,,	12.7.43	AGSS.383 (1962), IXSS.383 (1971); stricken 20/12/71.
SS.384	*Parche*	,,	24.7.43	AGSS.384 (1962); sold Zidell Explorations (Portland) . ./7/70 & scrapped.
SS.385	*Bang*	,,	30.8.43	
SS.386	*Pilotfish*	,,	30.8.43	Expended as target off Hawaii 16/10/48.
SS.387	*Pintado*	,,	15.9.43	AGSS.387 (1965); sold Zidell Explorations (Portland) 20/1/69 & scrapped.
SS.388	*Pipefish*	,,	12.10.43	AGSS.388 (1962); sold Zidell Explorations (Portland) 20/1/69 & scrapped.

Hull No.	Name	Builder	Launched	Fate
SS.389	*Piranha*	Portsmouth N.Y.	27.10.43	AGSS.389 (1962); sold Portsmouth Salvage Co. (Portsmouth) 11/8/70 & scrapped.
SS.390	*Plaice*	,,	15.11.43	Brazilian Navy *Bahia* (1963).
SS.391	*Pomfret*	,,	27.10.43	Turkish Navy *Oruc Reis* (1971).
SS.392	*Sterlet* (ex-*Pudiano*)	,,	27.10.43	Expended as target off .... 31/1/69.
SS.393	*Queenfish*	,,	30.11.43	AGSS.393 (1960); stricken 1/3/63 & expended as target.
SS.394	*Razorback*	,,	27.1.44	Turkish Navy *Murat Reis* (1970).
SS.395	*Redfish*	,,	27.1.44	AGSS.395 (1960); expended as target off San Clemente Isle 6/2/69.
SS.396	*Ronquil*	,,	27.1.44	Spanish Navy *Issac Peral* (1971).
SS.397	*Scabbardfish*	,,	27.1.44	R.H.N. *Triana* (1964).
SS.398	*Segundo*	,,	5.2.44	Stricken 8/8/70, disposal undetermined.

Hull No.	Name	Builder	Launched	Fate
SS.399	*Sea Cat*	Portsmouth N.Y.	21.2.44	AGSS.399 (1968); stricken 2/12/68 & expended as target.
SS.400	*Sea Devil*	,,	28.2.44	AGSS.400 (1960); expended as target off ..../../65.
SS.401	*Sea Dog*	,,	28.3.44	AGSS.401 (1962); stricken 2/12/68 & hulked for experimental work.
SS.402	*Sea Fox*	,,	28.3.44	Turkish Navy *Burak Reis* (1970).
SS.403	*Atule*	,,	6.3.44	AGSS.403 (1969), SS.403 (1971).
SS.404	*Spikefish*	,,	26.4.44	AGSS.404 (1962); stricken 1/5/63 & expended as target.
SS.405	*Sea Owl*	,,	7.5.44	SSK.405 (1963), AGSS.405 (19..); sold Universal Machinery Co. (Newton Center) 3/6/71 & scrapped.
SS.406	*Sea Poacher*	,,	20.5.44	AGSS.406 (1969), SS.406 (1971).
SS.407	*Sea Robin*	,,	25.5.44	Sold North American Smelting (Wilmington) 3/6/71 & scrapped.
SS.408	*Sennet*	,,	6.6.44	Stricken 2/12/68, disposal undetermined.

Hull No.	Name	Builder	Launched	Fate
SS.409	*Piper* (ex-*Awa*)	Portsmouth N.Y.	26.6.44	AGSS.409 (1967); stricken 1/7/70, disposal undetermined.
SS.410	*Threadfin*	,,	26.6.44	
SS.411	*Spadefish*	Mare Island N.Y. (Vallejo)	8.1.43	AGSS.411 (1964); sold Union Minerals & Alloys Corp. (New York) ../10/69.
SS.412	*Trepang*	,,	23.3.44	AGSS.412 (1962); expended as target off Southern California 16/9/69.
SS.413	*Spot*	,,	19.5.44	Chilean Navy *Simpson* (1962).
SS.414	*Springer*	,,	3.8.44	Chilean Navy *Thomson* (1961).
SS.415	*Stickleback*	,,	1.1.45	Collision with destroyer escort *Silverstein* 20m. south-west Pearl Harbour 29/5/58.
SS.416	*Tiru*	,,	16.9.47	Wrecked Frederick Reef 4/11/66, salved.

Machinery contracts: Engined by General Motors except *SS.292–312* and *381–416* by Fairbanks Morse (diesel engines); and by General Electric except *SS.292–312* and *381–416* by Elliot Motor (electric motors).

Hull No.	Name	Builder	Launched	Fate
SS.417	Tench	Portsmouth N.Y.	7.7.44	AGSS.417 (1969), SS.417 (1971).
SS.418	Thornback	,,	7.7.44	Turkish Navy Uluc Ali Reis (1971).
SS.419	Tigrone	,,	20.7.44	SSR.419 (1948), SS.419 (1959), AGSS.419 (1963).
SS.420	Tirante	,,	9.8.44	
SS.421	Trutta (ex-Tomatate)	,,	18.8.44	
SS.422	Toro	,,	23.8.44	AGSS.423 (1962); expended as target off Cape Cod 14/5/63, salved & sold North American Marine Salvage Co. (Bordertown, N.J.) . . /3/65 & scrapped.
SS.423	Torsk	,,	6.9.44	AGSS.423 (1968), IXSS.423 (1971); stricken 15/12/71.
SS.424	Quillback (ex-Trembler)	,,	1.10.44	
SS.425	Trumpetfish	Cramp Sbdg. (Philadelphia)	13.5.45	

"Tench" class: **AMBERJACK, ARGONAUT, CHICOLAR, COMBER, CONGER, CORSAIR, CUTLASS, DIABLO, DORADO, GRAMPUS, GRAYLING, GRENADIER, IREX, MEDREGAL, NEEDLEFISH, ODAX, PICKEREL, POMODON, POMPANO, QUILLBACK, REMORA, REQUIN, RUNNER, SARDA, SCULPIN, SEA LEOPARD, SEA PANTHER, SIRAGO, SPINAX, TENCH, THORNBACK, TIBURON, TIGRONE, TIRANTE, TORO, TORSK, TRUMPETFISH, TRUTTA, TURBOT, TUSK, ULUA, UNICORN (i), UNICORN (ii), VANDACE, VOLADOR, WAHOO (i), WAHOO (ii), WALRUS (i), WALRUS (ii), WHITEFISH, WHITING, WOLFFISH,** and **EIGHTY-TWO** units unnamed

The "Tench" class were designed to mount one 5in gun, again moved to abaft the conning tower, and one 40mm A.A. forward and one 20mm A.A. gun aft on the conning tower structure; but they were subsequently modified to ship a second 40mm A.A. in place of the 20mm A.A. gun, and in some units a second 5in/25cal A.A. deck gun was added forward of the conning tower.

Displacement:	1,570/2,428 except *SS.417–424* 2,416 and *SS.475–515* 2,414 tons.
Dimensions:	307(wl) 311$\frac{3}{4}$(oa) × 27$\frac{1}{4}$ × 15$\frac{1}{4}$ feet.
Machinery:	Two shafts; 10-cylinder Fairbanks Morse type 38D–1/8 except *SS.435–474* 16-cylinder General Motors type 278A diesel engines (two/shaft)/General Electric (in *SS.417–424* & *435–474*) or Elliot Motor (in *SS.425–434* & *475–520*) or Westinghouse (in *SS.521–550*) electric motors B.H.P./S.H.P. 5,400/2,740 = 20$\frac{1}{4}$/8$\frac{3}{4}$ knots.
Bunkers & radius:	O.F. 454 except *SS.435–474* 389 tons/252-cell Exide except *SS.424, 475, 476, 478, 480–483, 485* & *488* Gould battery; ..,...,/... miles @ ../.. knots.
Armament:	One 5-inch/25cal A.A., one 40mm A.A. (not in *SS.435–474*), one except *SS.435–474* two 20mm A.A. (1/2 × 1), two ·5-inch except *SS.435–474* ·3-inch A.A. (2 × 1) guns; ten 21-inch (six fwd & four aft—twenty-four torpedoes) T.T.
Complement:	80–90.
Diving depth:	400 feet.

Hull No.	Name	Builder	Launched	Fate
SS.426	*Tusk*	Cramp Sbdg. (Philadelphia)	8.7.45	
SS.427	*Turbot*	,,	. . . .	Cancelled incomplete and scrapped.
SS.428	*Ulua*	,,	. . . .	Cancelled incomplete and scrapped.
SS.429	*Unicorn* (i)	,,	—	Cancelled 29/7/44.
SS.430	*Vandance*	,,	—	Cancelled 29/7/44.
SS.431	*Walrus* (i)	,,	—	Cancelled 29/7/44.
SS.432	*Whitefish*	,,	—	Cancelled 29/7/44.
SS.433	*Whiting*	,,	—	Cancelled 29/7/44.
SS.434	*Wolffish*	,,	—	Cancelled 29/7/44.
SS.435	Corsair	Electric Boat (Groton)	3.5.46	AGSS.435 (1960); sold Peck Iron & Metal (Portsmouth) . . /10/68 & scrapped.
SS.436	*Unicorn* (ii)	,,	1.8.46	Partially completed only; sold Marlene Blouse Corp. (. . . . .) 27/8/59 & scrapped.
SS.437	*Walrus* (ii)	,,	20.9.46	Partially completed only; sold Marlene Blouse Corp. (. . . . .) 27/8/59 & scrapped.

As completed the ARGONAUT *had a 5-inch A.A. gun on deck aft and provision to ship a second 5-inch A.A. gun forward, while on the conning tower there was a 40 mm A.A. gun forward and a twin 20 mm A.A. mounting aft.*

Hull No.	Name	Builder	Launched	Fate
SS.438 to SS.457	Unnamed	Electric Boat (Groton)	—	Cancelled 29/7/44.
SS.458 to SS.463	Unnamed	Manitowoc Sbdg.	—	Cancelled 29/7/44.
SS.464	*Chicolar*	,,	—	Cancelled 29/7/44.
SS.465 to SS.474	Unnamed	,,	—	Cancelled 29/7/44.
SS.475	*Argonaut* (ii)	Portsmouth N.Y.	1.10.44	R.C.N. *Rainbow* (1968).
SS.476	*Runner* (ii)	,,	17.10.44	AGSS.476 (1969); IXSS.476 (1971); stricken 15/12/71.
SS.477	*Conger*	,,	17.10.44	AGSS.477 (1962); sold Peck Iron & Metal (Portsmouth) ../6/64 & scrapped.
SS.478	*Cutlass*	,,	5.11.44	
SS.479	*Diablo*	,,	1.12.44	AGSS.479 (1962), Pakistani Navy *Ghazi* (1964); sunk—cause unknown—Indian naval forces South Arabian Sea ../12/71.

Hull No.	Name	Builder	Launched	Fate
SS.480	*Medregal*	Portsmouth N.Y.	15.12.44	AGSS.480 (1969); expended as target off ..../8/70.
SS.481	*Requin*	,,	1.1.45	SSR.481 (1948), SS.481 (1959), AGSS.481 (1968), IXSS.481 (1971); stricken 20/12/71.
SS.482	*Irex*	,,	26.1.45	AGSS.482 (19..); sold North American Smelting (Wilmington) 13/9/71 & scrapped.
SS.483	*Sea Leopard*	,,	2.3.45	
SS.484	*Odax*	,,	10.4.45	
SS.485	*Sirago*	,,	11.5.45	Stricken 1/6/72.
SS.486	*Pomodon*	,,	12.6.45	Sold Nicolai Joffe Corp. (Beverly Hills) 28/12/71 & scrapped.
SS.487	*Remora*	,,	12.7.45	
SS.488	*Sarda*	,,	24.8.45	AGSS.488 (1962); sold North American Marine Salvage Co. (Bordertown, N.J.) ../3/65 & scrapped.
SS.489	*Spinax*	,,	20.11.45	SSR.489 (1948), SS.489 (1959), AGSS.489 (19..); stricken 11/10/69, disposal undetermined.

Hull No.	Name	Builder	Launched	Fate
SS.490	*Volador*	Portsmouth N.Y.	17.1.46	
SS.491	*Pompano* (ii)	,,	—	Cancelled 12/8/45 and scrapped on slip.
SS.492	*Grayling* (ii)	,,	—	Cancelled 12/8/45.
SS.493	*Needlefish* (ii)	,,	—	Cancelled 12/8/45.
SS.494	*Sculpin* (ii)	,,	—	Cancelled 12/8/45.
SS.495 to SS.515	Unnamed	,,	—	Cancelled 29/7/44.
SS.516	*Wahoo* (iii)	Mare Island N.Y. (Vallejo)	—	Cancelled 7/1/46 and scrapped on slip.
SS.517	Unnamed	,,	—	Cancelled 29/7/44 and scrapped on slip.
SS.518	*Wahoo* (ii)	,,	—	Cancelled 29/7/44.
SS.519 to SS.521	Unnamed	,,	—	Cancelled 29/7/44.

Hull No.	Name	Builder	Launched	Fate
SS.522	*Amberjack* (ii)	Boston N.Y.	15.12.44	
SS.523	*Grampus* (ii)	,,	15.12.44	Construction suspended 1945–48; stricken 13/5/72.
SS.524	*Pickerel* (ii)	,,	15.12.44	
SS.525	*Grenadier* (ii)	,,	15.12.44	
SS.526	*Dorado* (ii)	,,	—	Cancelled 29/7/44.
SS.527	*Comber*	,,	—	Cancelled 29/7/44.
SS.528	*Sea Panther*	,,	—	Cancelled 29/7/44.
SS.529	*Tiburon*	,,	—	Cancelled 29/7/44.
SS.530 to SS.536	Unnamed	Cramp Sbdg. (Philadelphia)	—	Cancelled 29/7/44.
SS.537 to SS.544	Unnamed	Boston N.Y.	—	Cancelled 29/7/44.

Hull No.	Name	Builder	Launched	Fate
SS.545 to SS.547	Unnamed	Electric Boat (Groton)	—	Cancelled 28/3/45.
SS.548 to SS.550	Unnamed	Portsmouth N.Y.	—	Cancelled 27/3/45.

Machinery contracts: Engined by Fairbanks Morse except *SS.435–474* General Motors (diesel engines); and *SS.417–424* and *435–474* by General Electric, *SS.425–434* and *475–520* by Elliot Motor, and *SS.521–550* by Westinghouse (electric motors).

Hull No.	Name	Builder	Launched	Fate
SS.551 to SS.555	Unnamed	Electric Boat (Groton)	—	Cancelled 26/3/45.
SS.556 to SS.560	Unnamed	Portsmouth N.Y.	—	Cancelled 26/3/45.
SS.561 and SS.562	Unnamed	Mare Island N.Y. (Vallejo)	—	Cancelled 26/3/45.

Machinery contracts: Not awarded.

Bureau 1944 design: **TWELVE** unnamed units.

In 1944 a fresh design was prepared to replace that of the fundamentally similar *Gato/Balao/Tench* types, which had rendered excellent service but were becoming outdated. To accommodate a higher surfaced speed and increased armament in the new design the hull was lengthened some 10/20ft with a corresponding rise in displacement. Two designs were drawn up: one with a length of 330ft to incorporate supercharged diesel engines for a speed of 22¼ knots surfaced, and another of 323½ft with naturally aspirated engines for a speed of 22 knots. Although authorisation to build was secured in February 1945, the project was abandoned the following month before any decision was reached on which alternative to adopt. An interesting feature of the design was the six small tubes for A/S torpedoes fitted externally forward of the conning tower and at 90deg to the centreline.

Displacement:	1,800 (2,100 full load)/2,700 tons.
Dimensions:	326(wl) 330(oa) × . . . × . . . feet.
Machinery:	Two shafts; diesel engines/electric motors B.H.P. 9,500/2,740 = 22¼/9¼ knots.
Bunkers & *radius:*	O.F. . . . tons/. . .-cell . . . . battery; . .,. . ./. . . miles @ . ./. . knots.
Armament:	One 5-inch/25cal A.A., two 40mm A.A. (2 × 1) guns; twelve 21-inch (six fwd & six aft—. . . . . torpedoes), six 12-inch (amid & external—six torpedoes) T.T.
Complement:	. . . .
Diving depth:	. . . feet.

Air attack	Surface attack	Submarine attack	Miscellaneous
(a) bombed	*(a) gunfire*	*(a) torpedoed*	*(a) unknown*
Sealion	S.44	Corvina	Grayling
Grayback*			Growler
Grenadier	Herring		Grunion
Gudgeon*		*(b) mined*	
	(b) depth charged	Pompano	Snook
Amberjack*	Argonaut	Swordfish‡	Kete
Halibut§			
Trigger*	Shark (i)	Albacore	*(b) in error*
Wahoo	Perch	Flier	S.25
Scamp*	Pickerel	Robalo	
Cisco*	Sculpin	Runner	Seawolf
Barbel	Swordfish‡	Scorpion	
Bullhead	Triton	Escolar	Dorado
	Trout		Tullibee
(b) torpedoed	Grampus	*(d) collision*	Tang
	Grayback*	S.26	
	Gudgeon*		*(c) foundered/wrecked*
			R.12
	Amberjack*	*(e) expended*	S.27
	Bonefish	S.16	S.28
	Trigger*	S.17	S.36
	Harder	S.37	S.39
Shark (ii)	Scamp*	S.38	
Golet	Capelin		Darter
Lagarto	Cisco*	Bass	Lancetfish†

* combination of air & surface attack: ‡ combination of surface & submarine attack: † later salved: § written off as constructive total loss

The 5-inch/25-cal. deck gun on the after deck of the SEADOG

[Photograph U.S. Navy

Hull No.	Name	

Hull No.	Name	

Hull No.	Name	

Hull No.	Name	

Hull No.	Name	

Hull No.	Name	

Hull No.	Name	

Hull No.	Name	

Hull No.	Name	

121

125